C000104599

Socialists in the trade unions

Alex Callinicos

Socialists in the trade unions

Alex Callinicos

London, Chicago and Melbourne

Socialists in the trade unions — Alex Callinicos
First published March 1995
Bookmarks, 265 Seven Sisters Road, London N4 2DE, England
Bookmarks, PO Box 16085, Chicago Il. 60616, USA
Bookmarks, GPO Box 1473N, Melbourne 3001, Australia
Copyright c Bookmarks

ISBN 1 898876 01 0

Printed by Cox and Wyman
Cover design by Ian Goodyer

The Socialist Workers Party is one of an international grouping of socialist organisations:
- **Australia:** International Socialists, PO Box A338, Sydney South NSW 2000
- **Belgium:** Socialisme International, Rue Lovinfosse 60, 4030 Grivengée, Belgium
- **Britain:** Socialist Workers Party, PO Box 82, London E3
- **Canada:** International Socialists, PO Box 339, Station E, Toronto, Ontario M6H 4E3
- **Cyprus:** Ergatiki Demokratia, PO Box 7280, Nicosia
- **Denmark:** Internationale Socialister, Postboks 642, 2200 København N, Denmark
- **France:** Socialisme International, BP 189, 75926 Paris Cedex 19
- **Germany:** Sozialistische Arbeitergruppe, Wolfgangstrasse 81, 6000 Frankfurt 1
- **Greece:** Organosi Sosialisliki Epanastasi, c/o Workers Solidarity, PO Box 8161, Athens 100 10, Greece
- **Holland:** International Socialists, PO Box 9720, 3506 GR Utrecht
- **Ireland:** Socialist Workers Movement, PO Box 1648, Dublin 8
- **Japan:** New Workers Tendency, PO Box 55, Tokorozawa Yubinkyoky, Sakana
- **New Zealand:** International Socialist Organization, PO Box 6157, Dunedin, New Zealand
- **Norway:** Internasjonale Socialisterr, Postboks 9226 Gronland, 0134 Oslo
- **Poland:** Solidarność Socjalistyczna, PO Box 12, 01-900 Warszawa 118
- **South Africa:** International Socialists of South Africa, PO Box 18530, Hillbrow 2038, Johannesberg
- **United States:** International Socialist Organisation, PO Box 16085, Chicago, Illinois 60616
- **Zimbabwe:** International Socialists, PO Box 6758, Harare

Contents

1. Are the unions finished? 7

2. Capitalism, the unions and
   union leaders 13

3. Rank and file movements 27

4. The last upturn: the 1960s and
   the early 1970s 41

5. Era of defeats: 1974-89 48

6. Tasks for today 54

7. Useful addresses 61

8. Notes 75

Acknowledgements

Many people's work has gone into this book. I would like to thank David Beecham, Tony Cliff, Chris Harman, Lee Humber, Mac McKenna and, especially, John Rees.

CHAPTER 1

Are the unions finished?

United we stand, divided we fall is the basic idea of trade unionism. It is an idea which remains as true today as it was on the day it was first coined. Wherever capitalism exists, and it dominates every corner of the modern world, workers join trade unions so that they can more effectively defend their jobs, wages and conditions.

Sometimes resistance is on a spectacular scale. The history of the last 15 years would be very different, and very much the worse for working people, without the struggle of the South African trade unions which were central to ending apartheid, the sacrifice of the trade unionists of Solidarity in Poland in the early 1980s which was key to undermining a brutal totalitarian regime, or the massive strike waves organised by the new unions in Brazil and South Korea. Workers' struggles have also played a major role in shaping the old heartlands of capitalism in central and western Europe. The Greek Tory government was broken by repeated general strikes organised by the unions in the early 1990s. In November 1994 one and a half million people marched through Rome as part of a protest organized by the three union federations against the right-wing government, an event central to the government's collapse a short time later.

Even in Britain, where the Tory government did inflict a number of serious defeats on the oldest, and still one of the strongest, trade union movements in the world during the 1980s, there are plenty of signs that the 1990s are seeing the beginnings of a revival in confidence and organisation. Trade union struggle is likely therefore to move back towards the political centre-stage. For anyone who is sick of the way today's society operates it is essential to understand how trade union struggle fits in to the broader objective of changing the world.

We cannot wish away the defeats suffered by workers in the late 1970s and 1980s, the drop in union membership, the fall in the number of strikes or the weakening of shop steward organisation which were their consequences. But neither should these setbacks be overstated. A careful look at the statistics reveals a far more optimistic picture than that painted by Tory politicians and too often accepted by Labour Party and trade union officials. For example, take the figures which claim to show that union members are a shrinking proportion of the workforce (a fall in 'union density', to use the statisticians jargon). Even the government's own Employment Department figures show that union density amongst workers remained steady at 35 per cent between 1992 and 1993. Moreover, union density in workplaces with more than 50 employees was much higher — 47 percent.

But these aren't the figures the Tories want us to look at. They try to focus attention on the figures which claimed that union density had fallen from 32 percent in 1992 to 31 per cent in 1993.[1] However, they don't point out that this measure includes the self-employed and people on government schemes. A similar abuse of statistics is to be found when we look at the figures for the overall decline in union membership. The Tories and the right wingers in the labour movement would have us believe that people are flooding out of the unions because they can't stand union militants and aren't interested in strike action. The truth is different. Most of the decline in union membership from its peak in the 1970s is actually due to growing unemployment. Not surprisingly, people who lose their jobs rarely remain members of a trade union. The government's own *Employment Gazette* admitted: 'the number of non-manual union members has been broadly stable over the past four years, whereas the number of manual union members has declined by more than one million or 25 per cent. The decline in membership overall since 1989 can thus be accounted for almost entirely by the decline in manual membership.'[2]

Another highly respected survey also admitted the following:

1. There is no evidence of an overall decline in either union membership or recognition or collective bargaining in workplaces employing over 200 employees — the larger workplaces.

2. Derecognition of unions is insignificant, with the exception of one or two sectors, notably printing and publishing.

3. There has been hardly any decline in workplace organization where bargaining was well-established — in some cases the reverse is true. The number of factories with joint stewards committees rose from a third to more than a half between 1984 and 1990.

4. The survey does not record any significant shift towards single union deals, no-strike agreements or non-union representation.[3]

Beneath the statistics lies the reality of workplace trade union organisation still entrenched in what remains of its old strongholds.

Often unemployment and the closure of manufacturing plants are treated as if they amounted to an irreversible decline of organized labour, or even the disappearance of the working class itself. But this is to confuse the working class with one particular kind of employment — blue collar, manual labour. In reality the working class consists of all those who are compelled to sell their labour power in order to earn a wage on which they can survive. Huge increases in productivity in manufacturing industry over the past fifty years mean that fewer workers can produce more goods. But at the same time the number of workers in service industries, both privately and publicly owned, has greatly increased. This is not an entirely new situation. Even in the 19th century, when we can properly start to talk about the working class as a distinct class the largest single group of workers in Britain was not miners or mill-labourers but domestic servants.

What is new about today's white-collar workers is that they do not work in isolation in private houses but in huge offices or supermarkets. Here they are increasingly subject to basically the same conditions of work as and often paid worse wages than manual industrial workers. The struggles of the early 1970s, most notably the strikes of miners, dockers, and engineering workers which eventually brought down the Tory government of Edward Heath, included the spread of militant trade unionism to public sector white-collar workers such as teachers and civil servants.

More recently, there have been signs of the same militancy being taken up by some white-collar workers in the private sector — for example, bank-workers have gone on strike, a previously inconceivable development.

But not all of the decline in union membership can be put down simply to unemployment. Part of this decline in is accounted for by the failure of unions to recruit enough workers in sectors that have expanded as the old manufacturing industries have shrunk. Responsibility for this failure lies fair and square at the door of the trade union leadership.

Throughout the 1980s and on into the 1990s the trade union leadership has been committed to a self-proclaimed strategy of 'new realism'. This saw union leaders turn their backs on traditional methods of trade union organisation, arguing to accept the stringent limitations of the trade union laws passed by the Tories and insisting, in the words of GMB leader John Edmonds, that unions could only attract new members by becoming 'service providers'. Glossy leaflets advertising credit cards and cheap insurance replaced active union recruitment and the kind of action that demonstrates the effectiveness of union organisation in defending workers living standards.

The great irony in all this was not simply that it did not work, but that it was not even what most union members wanted. A survey of nearly 3,000 new union members conducted in 1990 found that a mere 9.7 percent of white collar workers gave 'benefits and services (including financial services)' as one of their two main reasons for joining a union. Among manual workers the figure was 12.1 percent. Far more important to most white-collar workers were 'to support me if I had a problem at work' (71.9 percent), 'to improve my pay and conditions' (49 percent) and 'I believe in trade unionism and wish to take part' (24 percent).[4] Not surprisingly, when unions do take recruitment campaigns seriously they are successful. The Union of Shop, Distributive and Allied Workers (USDAW) has a hard time keeping its membership figures up because of the very nature of the workplaces it deals with. Only 13 percent of employees in the industry are in the union (although the figure is 24 percent in workplaces employing over 50 people). A high percentage of the workforce are part-timers and turnover is rapid. But after a determined recruitment campaign in 1990 108,294 new members joined the union, bringing the total percentage of shopworkers in the union that year up to 30 percent.[5]

Right wingers, and even some demoralised socialists, unconvinced by these arguments point to low strike figures as proof that the unions are in irreversible decline. It is true that strike figures are low — the number of strikes in 1993 was the lowest ever. But these figures underestimate the militancy bubbling under in the working class. For instance, the figures do not count strikes lasting less than a day, so ignoring the significance of brief stoppages. Neither do they measure strike action that has been prevented by union officials, or strike ballots in favour of action which are subsequently ignored by union leaders. They thus underestimate the anger and willingness to fight on the part of workers themselves.

Support for this analysis comes from a survey carried out in the summer of 1994 by the largest solicitors' Employment Law Department in the country. Their survey of 100 of the top 500 companies found 'a bleak picture for the future and perhaps even a return to seventies-style industrial relations . . . considerably more industrial tension bubbling under the surface than the simple "days lost" government statistics [indicates] . . . a surprising 22 percent [of firms] admitted industrial tension (strikes or action short of strikes) in the last 12 months'.[6]

The level of strike action is strongly influenced by the perpetual upward and downward movement of the capitalist economy. It should hardly be surprising that the threat of sackings which accompanied the economic slumps in the mid-1970s, early 1980s and early 1990s undermined British workers' confidence and therefore sharply reduced the level of strike activity. But the fall in unemployment during the short-lived 'Lawson boom' at the end of the 1980s led to a burst of strikes. The partial and limited economic recovery being experienced by Britain in the mid-1990s is likely to have a similar effect. This time militancy is also being fuelled by the deep popular distrust felt for the Tory government and very many of the central pillars of the establishment — the police, the courts, privatised industry and the monarchy to name only some of the more obvious cases.

However, any upsurge by workers will run up against the barrier created by the series of anti-union laws passed by the Tories since 1979, laws which, to its shame, Tony Blair's Labour Party plans to leave largely unchanged. Many trade unionists believe that the legal restraints now imposed on industrial action have made it impossible to wage effective strikes. This belief is strongly encouraged by trade-union officials seeking to firm up support for their 'new realism'. But experience shows both that it is one thing to pass anti-union laws but quite another to implement them, and that such laws can be taken on and defeated. What is required is that enough workers are willing to take industrial action in defiance of the law. This was the lesson of the dockers' struggle in 1972, when large-scale strike action freed five dockers from Pentonville prison and broke the Tory Industrial Relations Act under which they had been imprisoned.

Contrary to the arguments of the pessimists in the labour movement, the technological and organizational changes of the past 20 years can operate to workers' advantage. For example, during the 1980s the world's car firms adopted the Japanese 'just-in-time' system of keeping very low stocks of parts and materials. This reduces costs but makes the industry much more vulnerable to strikes. Thus in September 1994 11,500 workers at General Motors' Buick City complex in Flint, Michigan, went on strike in protest against the company's policy of increasing overtime rather than hire new workers to meet growing demand. The plant produces parts for many other GM plants. Almost immediately 22,000 workers were laid off by GM. Had the strike lasted a week, dozens of plants in North America and Western Europe would have had to be shut down. But after three days the company caved in and agreed to hire nearly 800 extra workers. A similar strike at Ford's Dagenham plant in Britain in 1988 had much the same effect on Ford's European plants. The result was similar too — a victory for the unions. The working class is strong, not weak. The real question is how will it use its power?

CHAPTER 2

Capitalism, the unions and trade union leaders

Workers have only one strength — their collective ability to withdraw their labour and so bring the capitalist system to a halt. The great attraction of trade union power and the reason why millions of workers join unions is that they provide the organisation that can make this power effective.

But the unions also have two fundamental limitations. In the first place they are not usually organisations of the whole class but of only a part of the class. They are *trade* unions and therefore mirror the divisions imposed on workers by the capitalist system — divisions between white and blue collar workers, between engineers and miners, between the unemployed and the employed. Secondly, the unions devote themselves to improving workers' conditions within the existing framework of the capitalist system, not to fighting for workers to take control of the system. To adapt a formulation of Karl Marx's, they combat the effects of capitalist exploitation, rather that striving to do away with the exploitation itself.

These two weaknesses lead to a third. Trade unionism, trade union leaders and, for most of the time, the majority of trade union members, accept that there is a sharp division between politics and economics. Put most crudely, this leads to an attitude

13

which sees unions concerned with the economic struggle over wages, conditions and the like, while the Labour party concerns itself with politics in parliament on workers' behalf. Going along with this idea often means the challenge of the organized working class is blunted. It encourages the belief that the class struggle between labour and capital is a non-political, economic and social issue and that workers' interests are best served through negotiation and reform rather than through the revolutionary transformation of society. It helps stop workers' moving on from demanding a better return from capitalism to challenging the very existence of capitalism as a social and economic system.

When struggles take place on a large scale it's easy to see how important these limitations can become in determining whether workers or the government and the bosses win out. For example, the threat of Solidarity in Poland in the early 1980s was such an explosive, potentially revolutionary challenge to the Stalinist regime there that no such distinction between economics and politics could easily be drawn. The regime not only denied the mass of the population the effective rights of citizenship but controlled the bulk of the economy. Fighting for a wage-increase was a challenge to the state. Where, however, the state is kept at arm's length from the direct struggle between workers and bosses, workers' struggles to improve their situation at work don't necessarily threaten the structure of society, so the division between politics and economics seems to have more basis in reality.

The separation of economics and politics finds its clearest expression where capitalist democracy prevails — in what are called the liberal democracies of Western Europe and North America. These involve institutions such as universal suffrage, regular elections, a multi-party system and the liberal freedoms (of speech, assembly, organization and so on). Liberal democracy extends to voting for a government but not to having any say in the running of the company that employs you. You can vote for who you like at election times, but the same people are still there in the board rooms of Shell, Unilever, BP, British Gas and every other company in the country.

Liberal democracy treats everyone as politically equal citizens. So, media mogul Rupert Murdoch has only one vote, the same as the print workers he employs in his non-union print works. But this formal equality hides the huge inequality in their wealth, power and political influence. Murdoch has power because he has capital,

14

his workers have no capital and, consequently, virtually no political influence.

Workers have always had to fight to win the right too vote, the right to free speech, the right to join trade unions and so on. These struggles are an important step in the development of the workers movement. As the great Russian revolutionary Leon Trotsky argued, capitalist democracy provides a framework within which workers can develop their own class organizations:

> In the course of many decades, the workers have built up within the bourgeois democracy, by utilizing it, by fighting against it, their own strongholds and bases of proletarian democracy: the trade unions, the political parties, the educational and sports clubs, the cooperatives etc.[1]

The other side to this relationship is that, while capitalist democracy permits the development of working-class organization (not simply trade unions but also the parties linked to the unions, like Labour in Britain), it also seeks to contain and to incorporate that organization. Many things determine whether such attempts at incorporation will succeed. A weak union movement and a right wing Labour Party will be more easily contained than a powerful, left wing labour movement. A union movement that has just scored a series of victories will be harder to blunt than one that has suffered a series of defeats. But more than any other single factor capitalist democracy's ability to contain the organized working class depends on economic prosperity. A rich and expanding economy is likely to have the capacity to grant improvements in working-class living standards. An ailing economy is less likely to be able to. If the trade-union struggle is unable to deliver increases in real wages, then workers are less willing to confine themselves within a capitalist framework.

The great waves of economic expansion which the capitalist system enjoyed in the mid-and late nineteenth century and more recently during the Long Boom of the 1950s and 1960s, provided the prosperity which saw both Labour and Tory governments granting reforms. In times of economic boom it is possible, thanks to rises in labour productivity and expanding demand for goods and services, simultaneously to increase both profits and real wages, temporarily escaping the bind which, Marx argued, drives bosses and workers into conflict with each other. But equally, periods of sustained and severe economic slump limit capitalists' room for manoeuvre and forces them to attack jobs, wages and conditions. These assaults often unleash class struggles which can no longer be so easily contained.

The trade union bureaucracy

There is one other crucial condition for the kind of trade unionism typical of the capitalist democracies — the existence of the trade-union bureaucracy, that is, of a social layer made up of full time officials with a material interest in confining the class struggle to the search for reforms within a capitalist framework. At the end of the nineteenth century Sidney and Beatrice Webb, co-authors of the Labour Party's Clause 4, were admiring the formation of a bureaucracy of full-time trade-union officials:

> during these years we watch a shifting of the leadership in the trade union world from the casual enthusiast and irresponsible agitator to a class of salaried officers expressly chosen out of the rank and file of trade unionists for their superior business capacity.[2]

Fifteen years later the sociologist Robert Michels detected the emergence of a similar layer of full-time officials in the German Labour Party, the SPD:

> There already exists in the proletariat an extensive stratum consisting of the directors of co-operative societies, the secretaries of trade unions, the trusted leaders of various organizations, whose psychology is entirely modelled upon that of the bourgeois classes with whom they associate.[3]

The 1920s saw the consolidation of the trade-union bureaucracy in Britain (and early signs of its willingness to collaborate with the state). This process was promoted by the rapid expansion of union membership during and after the Great War (2.6 million in 1914, 8.3 million in 1920), a series of amalgamations which led to the formation of such giant general unions as the Transport and General Workers Union (TGWU) and the National Union of General and Municipal Workers (NUGMW) — core of the modern General and Municipal Boilermakers union (GMB) — and the growth of national collective bargaining to replace the district settlements which had set wage rates before 1914.[4] The commitment of the TUC General Council to class collaboration was also fully demonstrated

16

early on when it hastily called off the General Strike of May 1926. After the strike the negotiations it pursued with top industrialists — the Mond-Turner talks — ensured an official strike call was not issued again until into the 1950s. In June 1940, with the appointment of the TGWU general secretary, Ernest Bevin, as Minister of Labour and National Service in Winston Churchill's coalition government the trade-union bureaucracy's incorporation into the state machine was formalized.[5]

The formation of a conservative labour bureaucracy is inherent in the very nature of trade unionism. The trade-union struggle is concerned with improving the terms on which workers are exploited, not with ending that exploitation. Confining the class struggle within the limits of capitalism presumes that the interests of labour and capital can be reconciled — that higher wages can be won without undermining profitability. The compromises that are forced on workers when the balance of class forces is against them are inevitable so long as the trade-union struggle is kept within the limits of capitalist society. Someone has to negotiate these compromises. Therefore, there is a pressure which encourages a division of labour between the mass of workers and their trade-union representatives. The latter's time is increasingly spent in bargaining with employers. Some of these representatives sooner or later become full-time workers for the union, paid out of members' subscriptions. The effect, whatever the beliefs of the officials, is to isolate them from those they represent.

Full-time officials are removed from the discipline of the shopfloor, from the dirt and dangers often found there, from the immediate conflicts with supervisor and manager, from the fellowship of their workmates, to the very different environment of an office. Even if they are not paid more than their members (and they usually are), their earnings no longer depend on the ups and downs of capitalist production — they no longer involve working overtime, nor are they vulnerable to short-time working. If a plant is closed the official who negotiates the redundancies will not get the sack. Constantly closeted with management, full timers come to see negotiation, compromise, the reconciliation of capital and labour as the very stuff of trade unionism. Struggle appears as a disruption of the bargaining process, a nuisance and inconvenience, which may threaten the accumulated funds of the union. The efficient running of the union machine becomes an end in itself, threatening even the limited goal of improving the terms on which the worker is exploited.

The great German revolutionary Rosa Luxemburg well described the political effects of 'the introduction of a regular trade union officialdom' in Germany after 1890:

> the naturally restricted horizon which is bound up with disconnected economic struggles in a peaceful period, leads too easily to bureaucratism and a certain narrowness of outlook. Both, however, express themselves in ... the overvaluation of the organization, which from being a means has gradually changed into an end in itself, a precious thing, to which the interests of the struggles should be subordinated. From this also comes that openly admitted need for peace that shrinks from great risks and presumed dangers to the stability of the trade unions, and the overvaluation of the trade-union method of struggle, its prospects and its successes.

Luxemburg also noted how this was accompanied by 'a revolution in the relations of leaders and rank and file', so that 'the initiative and power of making decisions ... devolve upon trade-union specialists ... and the most passive virtue of discipline upon the mass of members'.[6] The basic process was the same in all the advanced capitalist countries — the emergence of a distinctive social layer of full-time officials with interests different to those of the rank and file. Full timers are at the same time committed to the improvement of workers' conditions within the limits of capitalism but also reluctant to use even the weapons of economic class struggle for fear of disrupting their relations with the employers and endangering the stability and resources of their organisations.[7]

The conservatism of the trade-union bureaucracy has material, economic roots. Full time trade-union officials are an economically privileged group compared to the workers they represent. A recent study of trade-union officials in Britain showed that 61 percent of General Secretaries earned more than £30,000 per year in 1991.[8] In some cases the gulf is even wider. Alan Johnson, currently joint general secretary of the Communication Workers Union, receives a pay and perks package worth £72,570 a year, compared to the average of £14,000 earned by the postal delivery workers he represents. Sometimes lay officials and representatives are drawn into the same network of material privileges. Members of the executive council of the union of Rail, Maritime and Transport workers (RMT) are seconded to work full-time for the union during their three-year term, and are paid an annual 'allowance', usually worth £28,000.[9] These material privileges give the trade-union bureaucracy a stake in maintaining the capitalist society which grants them a role negotiating the terms on which workers are exploited. This in turn creates a conflict of interests between the full-time officials and rank and file workers who have an interest in reducing, and ultimately abolishing their exploitation by the bosses.

The struggles workers wage, even simply to wrest reforms out of the existing system, may threaten its stability. So again and again union leaders intervene to prevent these struggles from getting out of control and end them on terms which fall far short of their members' aspirations. The burning resentment these betrayals create among ordinary workers gives rise, in certain conditions (which we will look at more closely in the next chapter), to rank-and-file organizations which fight independently of the officials.

It is important to understand that while a full-scale trade-union bureaucracy tends to be found chiefly in rich countries like Britain and the US, the tendency towards the development of such a bureaucracy is inherent in any trade-union movement of any size. A good illustration is provided by the case of COSATU in South Africa. Independent unions were built in South Africa during the 1970s and 1980s on the basis of strong democratic control by the rank and file. Shop stewards, the workers' lay representatives, were given a key role in the new workers' movement which became increasingly involved in political struggles as time went on. But by the end of the 1980s, as the unions became more and more involved in national bargaining with the employers and the state, even a sympathetic history of COSATU was forced to acknowledge that 'it is usually union officials who wield real power, with elected worker leaders and executive committee acting as a check on the abuse of that power.'[10] So even militant trade unionism isn't immune to bureaucratic tendencies. These tendencies arise from the self-limiting nature intrinsic to trade unionism, its pursuit of a better life for workers within existing society.

Left and right officials

The conflict between bureaucracy and rank and file is the fundamental division inside the trade-union movement. However, many of the British left would dispute this claim. The Communist Party, the key political influence among left-wing trade unionists in Britain until it began to fall apart in the 1980s, argued from the mid-1920s onwards that the main division within the unions was the political one between left and right. Therefore, socialists should concentrate on getting left-wing officials elected. It was on this basis that the CP developed a strategy of building Broad Lefts. These operated essentially as electoral coalitions grouping left wingers together in order to support a left wing candidate in union elections. The CP no longer exists, but the Broad Left strategy is still very attractive to many trade union activists.

The analysis behind this strategy is, on the face of it, quite plausible. Plainly there are deep political divisions among the trade-union leaders. For example, miners' leader Arthur Scargill stands for a very different kind of trade unionism from that represented by right winger Bill Jordan of the Amalgamated Engineering and Electrical Union (AEEU). The most important union controlled by the left, the TGWU, can be counted on to stand up at TUC and Labour Party conferences and defend policies that are substantially different from those advocated by right-led unions such as the the AEEU. The real question, however, isn't whether these divisions exist, but whether they are more important than the interests binding all union officials together as a distinct social group. Quite contrary to its authors' own views, one recent study found:

> officers provided strong evidence of a desire to retain discretion and limit control by union members. For example, 74 per cent of officers reported that they preferred members and lay representatives to present them with 'open-ended' claims (e.g. a request for a 'substantial increase') and 75 per cent disagreed with the statement that, 'The full-time officer should always go along with the wishes of his/her members' . . . most officers were keen to preserve their negotiating discretion and escape from close control by members.[11]

The divisions among union officials are a consequence of the fact that trade unions are democratic mass organizations. Debates within unions reflect a variety of pressures: some of these involve the intervention of the bosses — usually through the agency of the mass media — in internal union politics. The right-wing leaders of the old electricians' union (now part of the AEEU) benefited considerably from the backing they received from the Tory press. Other pressures come from the rank and file. The battle to win unions for the left is often an echo of great class struggles. Arthur Scargill's election as president of the mineworkers' union in 1981 would have been inconceivable without the series of miners' strikes, official and unofficial, between 1969 and 1974 and his own role within them.

It is understandable enough that rank-and-file activists, impatient with betrayals by right-wing officials should believe that by replacing the latter with left-wingers drawn from their own ranks they can transform the unions into real fighting organizations. But this belief reflects a lack of self-confidence on the rank and file's part, since it invites them to rely on putting the right people at the top of the union rather than on using their own strength and organization. After all, the miners won their greatest victories, in the national strikes of 1972 and 1974, under the leadership of a right-wing president, Joe Gormley.

In any case, the differences between the left and right officials are less important than what unites them. Even the most radical left-wing leader is still part of the same social group as his or her right-wing counterparts — the union bureaucracy. This means that he or she is likely, at crucial junctures, to hold back the struggle, and to strike rotten compromises with the employers. At the end of the 1926 General Strike, the left wing of the TUC General Council headed by Alonzo Swales, A. A. Purcell, and George Hicks agreed with the right in calling off the strike and leaving the miners to fight on alone and suffer bitter defeat after a six-month lock-out. Once again, it was the two great leaders of the trade-union left, Jack Jones of the TGWU and Hugh Scanlon of the engineers, who played the key role in implementing a Social Contract with the 1974-79 Labour government that led to the biggest cut in real wages for a century.

Two factors weigh particularly heavily with all trade-union officials, whatever their political beliefs. One is the union machine itself — its organization, finances, etc. — which, as Luxemburg put it, they tend to see as 'an end in itself, a precious thing, to which the interests of the struggles should be subordinated'.[12] The succession of anti-union laws introduced by Tory governments after 1979 struck a shrewd blow by bringing the weight of the laws to bear chiefly onto union assets. It is an extremely rare union leader who is prepared to risk the union's funds in order to prosecute a strike. The National Union of Mineworkers' leadership was prepared to take this risk during the Great Strike of 1984-85, but it was shunned by the rest of the union bureaucracy which stood by while lawyers representing scab miners were allowed to seize NUM assets. Indeed, the main thrust of Tory anti-union legislation has been less to dismantle the trade unions than to strengthen the power of the full-time officials and give them an added incentive to intervene to prevent strikes by threatening their funds. A survey of managers showed that they only rarely actually used the law in industrial disputes. Rather, as one of them put it, 'legislation has led to a greater emphasis on the full use of avoidance-of-dispute procedures and involvement of full-time officials. In turn this has led to a more professional approach to establishing and maintaining agreements.'[13]

Union officials are also strongly influenced by a sense of collective responsibility which makes them reluctant to rock the boat. We can see this very clearly in the case of the most prominent left-wing trade unionist to have emerged since the early 1970s, Arthur Scargill. During the 1984-85 strike he strongly pushed for a far more militant prosecution of the dispute than the majority of the NUM executive was prepared to endorse. Yet he never broke publicly with the rest of the executive or encouraged rank-and-file miners to pursue the tactics that could win the strike in defiance of their officials. This allowed the powerful but conservative NUM Area leaderships — particularly that headed by Jack Taylor in Yorkshire — to sit on the strike, and allow it to gradually die from passivity and despair.[14]

Even more remarkable was Scargill's behaviour after the Tory government announced plans to close 31 pits in October 1992. There was an enormous explosion of popular anger. The pit-closures programme provided a focus for all the resentments that had been building up against an economy in recession and the mean and incompetent government presiding over it. Had a general strike been called then, the Tories would probably have fallen. Predictably enough the then TUC General Secretary, Norman Willis, marched firmly in the opposite direction, calling for a 'cooling-off period'. The TUC's policy was for protests — held jointly with the employers, then busy making tens of thousands of workers redundant. Yet Scargill did nothing to challenge this approach in deed or even in word. When groups of miners proposed to occupy pits threatened with closure, he intervened to stop this happening. The Tories were able to shut down even more pits than they had originally envisaged. After the event Scargill denounced the TUC for leaving the miners in the lurch. He was right about this — but he ignored his own failure to lead a real fight against the destruction of the mining industry.[15]

None of this means that the divisions within the trade-union bureaucracy are somehow irrelevant. Left officials are more likely to support better policies than right-wing ones. Their election is indicative of some willingness to fight on the part of the rank and file. Therefore socialists should support the trade-union left in its struggles with the right. This is different, however, from relying on any official, whatever his or her politics. Rank-and-file workers must look to themselves, and the organization and solidarity they are able to build, not to anyone at the top of the unions.

The trade union bureaucracy and the state

The trade-union bureaucracy provides the social base of reformist political parties. The Labour Party and its counterparts elsewhere, like the German SPD and the Socialist Parties of southern Europe, seek to reform capitalism, to make it a more democratic and humane system, while leaving its basis in the exploitation of the working class untouched. This corresponds closely to the pursuit of compromise between labour and capital that is the trade-union leaders' reason for existence.

Sometimes the link between union officialdom and reformist political organization takes a formal, institutional shape, as in the case of the block vote wielded by affiliated unions at Labour Party conferences (though this has been watered down by the introduction of one member, one vote, which gives MPs and members of constituency parties considerably more say than trade unionists in leadership elections). More usually, the connection is an informal one, but the alliance between union bureaucrats and reformist parliamentarians is no less real in countries like Germany than it is in Britain. [16]

Trade-union leaders are committed to the reform of capitalism, not its overthrow. If forced to choose between preserving the existing system and a revolutionary struggle against it, they will always choose the former. Tony Cliff provides a classic description of how union leaders — left and right alike — vacillate as a

23

consequence of their social position and of their ultimate loyalties in times of crisis and class confrontation:

> The union bureaucracy is both reformist and cowardly. Hence its ridiculously impotent and wretched position. It dreams of reforms but fears to settle accounts in real earnest with the state (which not only refuses to grant reforms but even withdraws those already granted) and it also fears the rank-and-file struggle which alone can deliver reforms. The union bureaucrats are afraid of losing their own privileges vis-a-vis the rank and file. Their fear of the mass struggle is much greater than their abhorrence of state control of the unions. At all decisive moments the union bureaucracy is bound to side with the state, but in the meantime it vacillates.[17]

A particularly clear example of the way in which the bureaucracy always comes down on the side of the existing state in times of crisis is provided by Britain in 1919. Some historians regard this year as the most dangerous year ever faced by British capitalism. Revolution in Europe, widespread industrial unrest, army mutinies, even a police strike: all of these seemed to threaten a ruling class gravely weakened by the First World War. This class, under the skillful leadership of the prime minister, David Lloyd George, nevertheless benefited from the unwillingness of the trade union bureaucracy to confront the state.[18] The Triple Alliance of mineworkers, railworkers, and transport workers threatened to strike in support of the miners' demand for the nationalization of the their industry. The left-wing Labour leader Aneurin Bevan describes the crucial meeting between the government and the leaders of the Triple Alliance, based on what Robert Smillie, secretary of the Miners' Federation and himself a prominent left-winger, had told him:

> Lloyd George sent for the labour leaders, and they went, so Robert told me, 'truculently determined they would not be talked over by the seductive and eloquent Welshman . . . He was quite frank with us from the outset,' Bob went on. 'He said to us: "Gentlemen, you have fashioned the Triple Alliance of the unions represented by you, a most formidable instrument. I feel bound to tell you that in our opinion we are at your mercy. The Army is disaffected and cannot be relied on. Trouble has occurred already in a number of camps. We have just

emerged from a great war and the people are eager for the reward of their sacrifices, and we are in no position to satisfy them. In these circumstances if you carry out your threat and strike, then you will defeat us.

"'But if you do so," went on Mr Lloyd George, "have you weighed the consequences? The strike will be in defiance of the Government of the country and by its very success will precipitate a constitutional crisis of the first importance. for if a force arises in the State that is stronger than the State itself, then it must be ready to take on the functions of the State, or withdraw and accept the authority of the State. Gentlemen," asked the Prime Minister quietly, "have you considered, and if you have, are you ready?" From that moment on,' said Robert Smillie, 'we were beaten and we knew we were.'[19]

Lloyd George had the trade-union leaders' measure. The strike was called off. The same pattern was at work during the General Strike of 1926. The TUC was pledged to strike in support of the miners, who were threatened with pay-cuts. The Tory prime minister, Stanley Baldwin, was intent on achieving a general reduction in wages. The General Council wanted to treat the issue as a trade-union dispute, without political overtones. Baldwin made it a constitutional question, depicting the General Strike as a challenge to the state (as indeed it was). Once it was posed in these terms the TUC's only thought was to flee the field of battle. Its attitude was summed up by the railwaymen's leader, J.H. Thomas: 'I have never disguised that, in a challenge to the Constitution, God help us, unless the government won. That is my view.'[20] No wonder that, under leadership of this calibre, the General Strike was soon called off and the miners deserted.

Nor is opting for the state a peculiarly British disease. One of the greatest upheavals in an advanced capitalist country came in France in May-June 1968, when a student revolt sparked off a massive general strike directed at the government of General Charles de Gaulle. It took the concerted efforts of the leaders of the CGT, the main union federation and members of the Communist Party to persuade the workers to end their strike in exchange for wage-increases and a general election.

The same pattern can be seen even in more politically unstable countries than Britain and France. Solidarity in 1980-81 was one of the greatest workers' movements in history, ten million workers democratically organized against the Polish state. But the union's leadership under Lech Walesa pursued a strategy they called 'self-limiting revolution', which involved seeking compromise between the working class and the Polish regime. Their reward was the imposition of martial law in December 1981, and the wholesale repression of Solidarity, a blow from which the union never recovered. The regime finally collapsed in 1989 because of its own internal weaknesses rather than as a result of the pressure of mass opposition.

The union bureaucracy's loyalty to the state is the clearest sign of the limitations of trade unionism — of its tendency to confine workers' struggles within the framework of the existing system by accepting a sharp separation between economics and politics. It underlines the need for a political organization which, rather than seeking reforms from the existing state, supports workers' struggles against that state. What is wanted is a political party of workers which seeks to replace the old system with a new form of state based on the democratic mass organizations of the working class. Building such a party is inseparable from the struggles that develop within the unions between bureaucracy and rank and file. Let's take a look at these struggles.

CHAPTER 3

Rank and file movements

R ank-and-file organizations are bodies of work place delegates subject to direct election and recall by the workers they represent. Both their workplace basis and the direct control of non full-time representatives by the rank and file distinguish these forms of organization from official trade-union structures. Official structures are usually organized on geographical rather than workplace lines and the full-time officials, even when they are elected rather than appointed, often hold office for life. Rank-and-file organizations, even though they usually exist within the official structures (and are sometimes closely integrated in them), arise directly from the daily struggle on the shop floor and often in conflict with the trade-union bureaucracy. Usually no-one plans their formation in advance.

The distance of trade-union officials from their members, and their commitment to class compromise inevitably brings them into conflict with the mass of trade unionists. The bureaucrats' betrayals of specific struggles make the rank and file aware of the clash of interests between themselves and their 'representatives' and therefore of the need for forms of organization more responsive to their own needs and wishes. Moreover, the centralized structure of trade-union officialdom and its isolation from the shop floor, can promote the growth of structures in the workplace able to react immediately to the everyday conflicts which arise. Situations where a significant portion of workers' earnings are fixed by local plant or shop bargaining will also encourage the

27

emergence of these structures.

The shop stewards in Britain are a classic example of rank-and-file organizations. They first emerged in the engineering industry in 1892 as agents of the district committees of the Amalgamated Society of Engineers (ASE), doing jobs like dues-collecting and signing on new members. However,

> shop stewards did not confine themselves to supplying information and undertaking organizational work on behalf of the District Committees. The tradition of workshop delegates serving on deputations to their employers continued, and the workshop deputation was a recognized part of the collective bargaining procedures.[1]

But if rank-and-file organizations tend to start from wage bargaining in the workplace they can in certain circumstances become organs of workers' power, challenging the authority of the capitalist state. The experience of the Russian Revolutions of 1905 and 1917 showed how workers' councils — what Russian workers called soviets — can develop out of the struggle in workplaces over partial economic demands. The first soviet was formed in St Petersburg in 1905 out of a strike by typesetters who wanted to be paid for setting punctuation marks. It developed into a rival government to the Tsar's, organizing an insurrectionary general strike. Trotsky, the president of the St Petersburg soviet, wrote:

> The soviet appears most often and primarily in connection with strike struggles that have the perspective of revolutionary development, but are in the given moment limited merely to economic demands ... soviets [are] that broad and flexible organizational form that is accessible to the masses who have just awakened at the very first of their revolutionary upsurge; and which is capable of uniting the working class in its entirety, independent of the size of that section which, in the given phase, has already matured to the point of understanding the task of the seizure of power.[2]

The great Italian revolutionary, Antonio Gramsci, saw that rank-and-file organizations could become organs of workers' power. He did so on the basis of the experience of Italy in 1918-20, the so called *biennio rosso*, when two years of revolutionary struggle saw workers shake society from top to bottom. At the centre of this social and political earthquake were the metal-

28

workers of Turin. They turned their shop stewards' committees — the internal commissions — from bodies for defending the privileges of skilled craftsmen into committees of factory delegates uniting skilled and unskilled, trade unionists and non trade unionists, who increasingly sought to assert their control over production. Gramsci argued:

> Today the internal commissions limit the power of the capitalist in the factory and perform functions of arbitration and discipline. Tomorrow, developed and enriched, they must be organs of proletarian power, replacing the capitalist in all his useful functions of management and administration.[3]

However, if rank-and-file organizations have the potential to become the basis of workers' councils, there is nothing inevitable about this happening. Indeed, rank-and-file organizations may not develop at all when union organization is weak or when the control of the full-time officials is tight — shop stewards in the United Autoworkers in the US are appointed rather than elected for example. In Britain the strength and militancy of shop stewards' organization have varied considerably depending on the shifting balance of power between labour and capital.

Equally, it is only in certain very specific conditions that rank-and-file organization and revolutionary socialist politics converge. The politics of rank-and-file organizations are usually far from revolutionary. This is inevitable since these workplace organizations, just like unions generally, start by seeking to win material improvements for particular groups of workers within the framework of capitalism. It is only in periods of economic and social crisis, when the employers and the state are forced to attack rank-and-file organizations, that the workers involved in them are led to think in class rather than sectional terms.

In such circumstances rank-and-file *movements* can emerge which are concerned to fight on the more general class front and to link together workers in different localities and industries. Such movements are usually led by revolutionary socialists, since it is only they who can give rank-and-file organizations the necessary political independence of both the bosses and the bureaucracy.

Table 1 British strike statistics; annual averages 1900-1993

	Number of strikes	Workers involved (000s)	Number of strikes (000s)
1900-1910	529	240	4,573
1911-13	1,074	1,0347	20,908
1914-18	844	632	5,292
1919-21	1,241	2,108	49,053
1922-25	629	503	11,968
1926	323	2,734	162,233
1927-32	379	344	4,740
1933-39	735	295	1,694
1940-44	1,491	499	1,816
1945-54	1,791	545	2,073
1955-64	2,521	1,116	3,889
1965-69	2,380	1,208	3,951
1970	3,906	1,793	10,980
1971	2,228	1,171	13,551
1972	2,497	1,722	23,909
1973	2,873	1,513	7,197
1974	2,922	1,622	14,750
1975	2,282	789	6,012
1976	2,016	670	3,284
1977	2,703	1,155	10,142
1978	2,471	1,003	9,381
1979	2,080	4,583	29,474
1980	1,348	834	11,964
1981	1,344	1,513	4,226
1982	1,538	2,103	5,314
1983	1,364	574	3,754
1984	1,221	1,464	27,135
1985	903	791	6,402
1986	1,074	720	1,920
1987	1,016	887	3,546
1988	781	790	3,702
1989	701	727	4,128
1990	630	298	1,903
1991	369	176	761
1992	253	148	528
1993	211	385	649

Sources: R. Hyman, Strikes, (London, 1977), and Employment Gazette (figures for 1980 onwards based on stoppages in progress).

The Great Unrest and the first shop stewards movement

The years between 1910 and 1921 saw a sharp escalation in the industrial struggle in Britain (see Table 1)[4]. Out of this came the first real rank-and-file movement. Before the First World War British capitalism was under severe pressure from rising industrial powers like Germany and the United States. In response to this pressure employers sought to restructure production, attacking wages and conditions. In industries like mining and engineering this involved a formidable offensive against the workers. It was in these conditions that shop stewards' organization began to develop into a real force. The employers' offensive provoked, a huge explosion of workers' struggles, the Labour Unrest of 1910-14.

The two most immediate characteristics of the unrest were mass strikes and rapid union recruitment. From 1910 until the outbreak of war, working days lost rose to an annual total of 10 million, while union membership increased from 2.1 million to 4.1 million over the same period.[5] The trade-union movement grew as a result of intense industrial struggles. First came bitter, largely unofficial strikes in the South Wales coalfield in 1910-11. The summer of 1911 saw fierce seafarers' and dockers' strikes in a number of cities and the first national railway strike. These were followed by a national miners' strike in the winter of 1911-12 and a strike by London transport workers the next summer.

The most notable feature of the Labour Unrest was the high degree of aggressive, sometimes violent and often unofficial industrial militancy. The strikers again and again clashed with both their own trade-union officials and with the forces of the state. Thus during the general transport strike on Merseyside in August 1911 the city authorities formed a committee of public safety and brought 3,000 troops and several hundred police into the city. Gunboats patrolled the Mersey to intimidate the strikers. The strike united the working class of Liverpool. The sectarian division between Protestants and Catholics, whipped up at that time by the pro-Tory Orange Order, was temporarily forgotten. One striker remembered that on the great demonstration of 13 August, when 80,000 workers took to the streets, 'the Garston band had walked five miles and their drum-major proudly whirled his sceptre twined with orange and green ribbons as he led his contingent band, half out of the Roman Catholic, half out of the local

31

Orange band.' On that day — known on Merseyside as Bloody Sunday — police and troops brutally broke up the march. But the working class of Liverpool fought back. The *Times* described 'guerrilla warfare' raging during the days that followed. In one neighbourhood 'the crowd erected barbed wire entanglements on a scientific scale and entrenched themselves behind barricades and dustbins and other domestic appliances.'[6]

Workers were thus being driven into conflict with the state itself. Moreover, a minority were so embittered by the failure of the trade-union leaders to support their struggles that they began to look for ways of using workers' growing industrial power directly to challenge the very existence of capitalism. Syndicalism grew in influence during the Labour Unrest. The syndicalists sought to transform the existing, still mainly craft unions into industrial unions each organizing all the workers in a particular industry as the basis of a workers' state.

The outbreak of the First World War in August 1914 caused a temporary abatement in industrial militancy and indeed there was a sharp fall in strikes during the war. Like their counterparts in the rest of Europe, the leaders of the Labour Party and the TUC supported their own state's war effort. In March 1915, the Amalgamated Society of Engineers and other unions concluded the Treasury Agreement with Lloyd George, the Liberal Chancellor of the Exchequer. Under this union leaders accepted 'dilution' — the introduction of unskilled workers to do jobs previously done by craftsmen — in order to increase war production. Pressure brought on by this agreement and by war time wages and conditions radicalized many engineering workers. A number of major industrial centres, most notably Glasgow and Sheffield, saw bitter struggles in the engineering industry. These gave birth to the Shop Stewards' and Workers' Committee Movement. This first rank-and-file movement was based on the Workers' Committees formed on the Clyde, in Sheffield and elsewhere and brought together shopfloor representatives from many different unions and industries to co-ordinate their struggles.[7]

The shop stewards' leaders were, in the main, revolutionary socialists of one variety or another — men like J.T. Murphy and Willie Gallacher who were later to play a leading role in the Communist Party. Their supporters, however, were mostly skilled engineering workers concerned to resist the erosion of craft privilege. The largest of the strikes called by the SS and WCM, those of May 1917 involving 200,000 engineering workers in 48 towns, succeeded in stopping the extension of dilution to work on private contracts. But the attempt by the leaders of the movement to focus on political issues by calling a national anti-war strike was an ignominious failure.

Nevertheless, the wartime shop stewards' movement represented an extremely important political step forward in two respects. First, the revolutionary stewards developed the theory of independent rank-and-file organization within the unions. Previously, revolutionary socialists had either refused to involve themselves in the unions at all or had sought, like the syndicalists, to replace them or transform them into revolutionary industrial unions that would grow to become a socialist state. The practical experience of building the wartime shop stewards' movement led its leaders to concentrate on developing within the official structures, rank-and-file organizations capable of fighting independently of the trade-union bureaucracy.

The shop stewards movement's attitude to the bureaucracy was summed up in the Clyde Workers' Committee's first leaflet, in November 1915. It remains the best summary of the nature of rank-and-file organization:

> We will support the officials just so long as they rightly represent the workers, but we will act independently immediately they misrepresent them. Being composed of delegates from every shop and untrammelled by obsolete rule or law, we claim to represent the true feeling of the workers. We can act immediately according to the merits of the case and the desire of the rank and file.[8]

Secondly, after the Russian Revolution of October 1917 the leaders of the shop stewards' movement began to see the Workers' Committees as soviets in embryo. The SS and WCM's paper argued in February 1919 that 'the Soviet Government of Russia sprung from the Workers' Committees, from the unofficial rank-and-file movement of the Russian people. The shop stewards are the first stage in the Soviet development.'[9] But if the revolutionary stewards came to see the political potential of rank-and-file organization, they were not so quick to draw another lesson of the Russian Revolution. The soviets had come to power under the leadership of the Bolshevik party. The stewards were slow to see how a revolutionary socialist party acted

33

to overcome the divisions inside the working class, linking together different struggles and focusing them on the battle, not simply with individual employers, but with the capitalist state itself.

The National Minority Movement and the General Strike

The October Revolution was an inspiration to socialists everywhere. In 1919 the Bolsheviks launched the Communist International (or Comintern) to advise and assist revolutionaries world-wide. The Comintern was instrumental in bringing together the various fractions of the British revolutionary left and the leaders of the SS and WCM to form the Communist Party of Great Britain in 1920. Pre-war British revolutionaries had seen socialist political organization essentially as a means of spreading ideas. The Bolsheviks' conception was very different. As the 'Theses on Tactics' adopted by the Comintern in 1921 argued:

> Communist Parties can only develop in struggle. Even the smallest Communist Parties should not restrict themselves to mere propaganda and agitation. They must form the spearhead of all proletarian mass organizations, showing the backward and vacillating masses, by putting forward practical proposals for struggle, by urging on the struggle for all the daily needs of the proletariat, how the struggle should be waged, and thus exposing to the masses the treacherous character of all non-communist parities. [10]

But the British Communist Party was formed against a background that was in many ways unfavourable to revolutionary hopes. The First World War ended in a sharp rise in the level of economic class struggle (see Table 1 on page 30). But by the time the CP was formed in 1920 the initiative had passed to the employers. Trade-union membership tumbled as the bosses went on the offensive. Numbers slipped from 8.3 million in 1920 to 5.6 million two years later, and by 1933 reached a low of 3.3 million.[11] The struggles of this period saw workers in retreat. Miners were locked out and defeated after six months in 1926. Engineers had already been locked out and beaten in 1922 while strikes by textile workers between 1929 and 1933 were beaten. The impact of these defeats on rank-and-file organization was drastic. J. T.

Murphy told the Fourth Congress of the Comintern in 1922:

> In England we have had a powerful shop stewards' movement.
> But it can and only does exist in given objective conditions. The
> necessary conditions at the moment in England do not exist.
> How can you build factory organizations when you have
> 1,750,000 workers walking the streets? You cannot build fac-
> tory organizations in empty and depleted workshops, while
> you have a great reservoir of unemployed workers.[12]

It was in this unpromising situation that the National Minority Movement (NMM) was launched in 1924 based on previous
Minority Movements in specific industries such as mining and engineering. The idea behind the NMM was explained by one Bolshevik leader, Lozovsky, at the Fourth Comintern Congress: 'The
aim here must be to create a more numerous opposition trade
union movement.' The CP was to 'act as a point of crystallization
round which the opposition elements will concentrate' and 'grow
concurrently with the growth of the opposition'.[13]

The NMM's aim was to rally the 'opposition elements' inside
the unions. But where were these elements to be found — at the
top of the movement or among the rank and file? CP leaders did
warn against trusting too much in left-wing trade union leaders:
'it would be a suicidal policy', wrote J.R. Campbell in October
1924, 'for the Communist Party and the Minority Movement to
place too much reliance on what we have called the official left
wing.' [14] But the main thrust of NMM strategy was indeed to look
to the top of the movement and elect and support left-wing trade-
union officials. Willie Gallacher wrote in September 1923:

> The movement that is springing up all over the country . . . is
> not a rank-and-file movement, but rather it is one that reaches
> through every strata of the trade unions. The driving force
> must necessarily come from the rank and file, but we should
> never forget that local officials, district officials, and national
> officials (a few of them at any rate) have never been led away
> by the desire to settle the troubles of capitalism.[15]

The best cure for the betrayals by right-wing leaders was to replace them with left-wingers. Arthur Horner, the Communist
miners' leader, even proposed that:

> The National Minority Conference . . . pledges the NMM and

all its supporters throughout the country to unceasingly work in the respective trade unions for the concentration of trade-union power in the General Council of the TUC, and the alteration of the constitution of the General Council to admit the best, wisest and most aggressive fighters on behalf of the working class as members.[16]

The fruits of this policy became clear in the General Strike of 1926. A revival in workers' combativity after the postwar slump was marked by the miners' success in winning a ten per cent wage rise in 1924. The NMM led a 'Back to the Unions' campaign to revive union membership. Economic recovery in 1923-4 and the consequent fall in unemployment gave workers greater confidence to take on the employers. On 'Red Friday', 31 July 1925, the government and the mine owners withdrew an attempt to cut miners' wages in face of a threatened general strike. But the prime minister, Baldwin, told the miners' leaders that 'all the workers of this country have to take reductions in wages to help put industry on its feet.'[17] Confrontation had only been postponed. The crunch came in May 1926.

Meanwhile, the revival in workers' militancy was reflected in the emergence on the TUC General Council of an articulate and verbally very militant left wing — notably Swales, Purcell, and Hicks — whose revolutionary rhetoric dominated the Trade Union Congresses of 1924 and 1925. The influence of the NMM grew rapidly during this period, especially in engineering and mining. The left-wing mood led to the TUC's participation in an Anglo-Russian Trade Union Committee set up in the spring of 1925. But when Baldwin finally manoeuvred the General Council into calling a general strike on 3 May 1926, the strike was tightly controlled from the top, with no scope given to rank-and-file initiative and called off on the flimsiest of pretexts after nine days, leaving the miners in the lurch. The CP and the NMM played a minor role, in part because their strategy was simply to call for support for the TUC left. One of the slogans raised by the CP during the strike was 'All Power to the General Council'. Two days before the outbreak of the General Strike J. T. Murphy of the CP described Swales and company as 'good trade-union leaders who have sufficient character to stand firm on the demands of the miners'.[18] But if this were true, why should workers bother to look to the CP rather than the much bigger forces of the TUC?

Within two weeks events proved Murphy's assessment of the TUC disastrously wrong. The 'good trade-union leaders' sold the miners down the river as readily as Ernest Bevin, J.H. Thomas or any other right winger on the General Council. One right winger, Ben Turner, protested in response to Communist criticism of the TUC's betrayal of the miners: 'the absolute unanimity of the General Council in declaring the General Strike off did not divide us into left-wingers and right-wingers.'[19]

The British CP's theoretical and political inadequacies were brutally exposed by the General Strike. But these weaknesses were underpinned by the effects of the degeneration of the Russian Revolution. By the mid-1920s Stalin and the bureaucracy he had built around him had displaced the soviets as the effective leadership in the Soviet Union. This bureaucracy placed its own interests and that of the state it controlled ahead of those of the world working class — a stance summed up by Stalin's slogan 'Socialism in One Country'. The Comintern was transformed into an instrument of Soviet foreign policy. The Anglo-Russian Trade Union Committee was diplomatically useful to Stalin, Zinoviev, and the other Comintern leaders. They were therefore reluctant to antagonize their allies in the TUC and so did nothing to correct the British CP's errors.

The Communist Party and the revival of shop stewards organization

The working-class movement began to recover from the disaster of the General Strike in the mid-1930s. This revival saw the beginnings of a change in the pattern of the economic class struggle that was to prevail until the late 1960s. As Table 1 shows, the number of strikes rose over the period to historically very high levels. At the same time, the number of workers involved in an 'average strike' in the 1960s was half that in the 1920s. The length of strikes also fell sharply.[20]

These changes reflected the emergence of strong shop stewards' organizations. The new rank-and-file organizations began to develop in the 1930s in some of the new industries like vehicle manufacture, electrical engineering, chemicals, and artificial fibres production, reflecting a reorganization of British capitalism away from old staple industries like coal and textiles.[21] By the mid-1930s the worst of the Great Depression was over. At the same

37

time, the prospect of another world war led the British government to launch a programme of rearmament which benefited not only industries producing directly for the military, such as the aircraft industry, but the whole of the engineering sector. The resulting fall in unemployment began to increase workers' self-confidence. The historian Richard Croucher writes:

> The effect of seeing old mates, even in ones and twos, coming back into the shops, was out of all proportion to the numbers involved. The iron workshop discipline of the previous two years, when it was not unheard of for men to be sacked for laughing at work, slowly began to dissipate.[22]

Nevertheless, it took a hard fight to organize the new industries. For example, the Pressed Steel plant at Cowley in Oxford involved highly automated, dangerous production. The workforce were unskilled and unorganized, consisting largely of 'immigrants' from high-unemployment areas in Wales, Scotland, and Ireland, and of locally recruited women. 'Workers were often hired and sacked by the day, unable to keep up with the pace required by a driving management.' In 1934 these 'coolies' (as they called themselves) rebelled against the 'slave shop' and, with the support of the TGWU and local Communists (but not the craft unions in the factory), launched a successful strike for higher wages and the right to shop-steward representation. By March 1938 there were 40 TGWU stewards at Pressed Steel representing 2,500 members.[23]

As Croucher observes, 'upsurges in the British labour movement, in the 1880s, 1910s, and again in the 1930s, brought an almost entirely unexpected broadening in membership, with previously thought to be among the most "backward" sections of the working class exploding into incandescent militancy.' Thus engineering apprentices, low-paid and denied proper training, launched two strike waves in 1937. The first began on the Clyde in April, and rapidly spread to other areas. Over 150,000 engineering workers took part in a one-day solidarity strike with the apprentices. Later that year, more strikes started in the Manchester area and spilled over elsewhere. The employers made some concessions nationally and many local wage agreements conceded big increases. More importantly, the strikes marked 'a watershed between the dark years of the Depression and the growing strength and confidence evident in the months immediately preceding the war' and a further strengthening of shop steward organisation.[24]

The revival of workplace trade-union organization was not simply a matter of piecemeal struggles by individual militants in different factories and industries. The Communist Party acted as a political driving force behind the growth of the stewards movement. Its members were among the best fighters organizing inside individual factories. At the same time the Communists sought to link together different workplaces in a movement capable both of supporting particular struggles and pursuing a coordinated strategy.

In March 1935 workers at Hawker's Brockworth factory came out on strike with strong support from the company's Kingston plant. Though the strike did not achieve all its objectives:

> it was the midwife of the first shop stewards' movement worthy of the name since that of the First World War. The strike occurred in the factories that formed the core of the most important aircraft firm. The Communists were able to use their network of contacts nationally to coordinate join action and organize support. The CP members had carefully prepared the way for the dispute in both Hawker factories, as well as in the unions themselves. The *Daily Worker* [the CP's newspaper] had been adopted as the official organ of the strike committee, and Tom Roberts, the CP's Industrial Organizer in the Midlands, had been involved throughout. The CP ensured that these advantages were not lost, and acted very quickly to set up a national movement of aircraft stewards.[25]

Soon after the Hawker strike the Aircraft Shop Stewards' National Council was set up. Its paper, *New Propellor*, developed from a support sheet produced during the strike, and was edited by a CP member. By October 1938 *New Propellor* claimed a circulation of 20,000 in 51 factories. The involvement of more and more factories in defence production, especially after the outbreak of the Second World War, helped to spread this movement beyond the aircraft industry. In April 1940 the Council became the Engineering and Allied Trades Shop Stewards' National Council at a conference attended by 283 shop stewards from 107 factories, by no means all of which were making aircraft.[26]

The Communist Party was transformed by its involvement in building shop stewards' organization. The change in the party is well described by Bob Darke, who was an important CP activist in Hackney and a leading militant first among the London firefighters

39

and then the bus-workers in the 1930s and 1940s. Darke joined the CP in 1931 but broke with the Party at the height of the Cold War in the 1950s. In 1931 the Party in Hackney was 'a loose gathering of two dozen intellectual wastrels', 'a little society of cafe-revolutionaries' who 'talked and talked'. Persistent involvement in the local working-class movement changed all this:

> When I started active work for the Party I began to enlist working-men like myself, paintworkers at first for I was then working for Lewis Bergers. Factory groups of Communists came into being, then cell fractions inside the unions ... The Zinken Cabinet Factory had the biggest Party membership. There were soon 20 Communists among the Dalston busmen. Bergers, when I left the factory, had 20 active comrades.
>
> By the time the war broke out we had our fingers in everything. We were a party of working-men and we were a dangerous party, aggressive, militant trade unionists, tried, tough, ruthless.[27]

When Darke left the CP in 1951 it had 880 members in Hackney, and had at some stage controlled 28 of the 35 union branches in the borough.[28] This growth in the CP's size and influence reflected the consistent work carried out by its members in the life and struggles of the working class of Hackney. Regular sales of the *Daily Worker* outside workplaces played a crucial role in building the CP. The same story could be told of many other working-class areas in Britain during the 1930s and 1940s.

However, there were serious weaknesses with the way the CP sought to rebuild workers' organization. The CP resolutely pursued a policy of trying to get left-wing union officials into union positions as the main way forward for workers. Already in the late 1930s the CP-led shop stewards' movement was seeking to find an 'accommodation' with the leadership of the Amalgamated Engineering Union (AEU), an approach which was reinforced by the elections of Jack Tanner, a former supporter of the NMM, as AEU President in 1939 and of the Communist Wal Hannington as National Organizer in 1942. The German invasion of the USSR in June 1941 brought the CP behind Britain's war effort. Its stewards opposed strikes and worked with management in Joint Production Committees. When workers' discontent found expression in a strike-wave in 1943-44, they sometimes turned to Trotskyist groups which, though tiny, supported their struggles.[29]

40

CHAPTER 4

The last upturn: the 1960s and the early 1970s

The full employment brought by the Second World War continued afterwards thanks to the long period of economic expansion of the 1950s and 1960s. These favourable economic conditions gave workers the bargaining power on the basis of which shop stewards' organization flourished. By the early 1970s there were 200,000 shop stewards in Britain, a third of them in engineering.[1] They were able to use the conditions of full employment to push up wages plant by plant. This shift in power to the shop floor was reflected in the fact that most strikes were unofficial.

Shop steward organisation during this period operated on the basis of what Tony Cliff and Colin Barker have called 'do-it-yourself reformism'. On the one hand, the authors point out, 'the shop stewards' organizations are largely restricted to the narrow horizon of economic, trade-union demands.' Moreover, they worked on a fragmented, shop by shop basis. On the other hand, the shop stewards' reformism was very different from the traditional reformism of the Labour party, which tells workers to rely on their MPs and union leaders to do things for them. Instead, the 1960s and 1970s saw workers 'doing things for themselves . . . growing in self-confidence and growing in their ability to run things for themselves'.[3]

The attempts by the employers and the state to break, or at least control the shop stewards forced the stewards to broaden their political horizons. The result, in the late 1960s and early 1970s, was the biggest class confrontations for half a century.[4] Under increasing pressure from foreign competitors, British capitalism could no longer easily afford to grant increases in real wages. Instead, living standards had to be forced down if the decline in the rate of profit was to be halted. The succession of crises which began to afflict the world economy in the late 1960s reduced the scope for concessions even further.[5]

The first assault on shop floor organization, mounted by the Labour government of 1964-70, failed in the face of a wave of public-sector strikes in 1969-70. It was left to Edward Heath's Conservative administration elected in June 1970 to resume the offensive. The Heath government's Industrial Relations Act and its succession of incomes policies provoked the largest and most political strikes since the 1920s. Thus 1972 saw a miners' strike which smashed Heath's first attempt to impose a national pay-limit, national stoppages in the railways, docks and building industries; factory occupations by Manchester engineering workers and a wave of unofficial action which forced the release of five dockers' stewards gaoled for defying the Industrial Relations Act. A second miners' strike in February 1974 delivered the final blow, not merely to Heath's second pay-limit but to the government itself.

One historian called the struggles under Heath 'the most extraordinary triumph of trade unionism in its long conflict with government':

The Labour Unrest of 1970-74 was far more massive and incomparably more successful than its predecessor of 1910-14. Millions of workers became involved in campaigns of civil disobedience arising out of resistance to the Government's Industrial Relations Act and to, a lesser extent, its Housing Finance Act. Over 200 occupations of factories, offices, workshops and shipyards occurred between 1972 and 1974 alone and many of them attained all or some of these objectives. Strikes in the public services became more frequent and prolonged. Some of them began to exhibit an ominous concern with the conditions of distribution as well as production. (Thus, some health service employees refused to supply privileges for private patients in public hospitals.)

But it was the coal miners, through their victories in the two Februaries of 1972 and 1974 which give a structure, a final roundedness and completeness which their contribution of 1912 had failed to supply to the earlier experience. First they blew the Government 'off course', then they landed it on the rocks. First, they compelled the Prime Minister to receive them in 10 Downing Street — which he had sworn he would never do — and forced him to concede more in 24 hours than had been conceded in the past 24 years. Then two years later their strike led him to introduce the three-day week [Heath reacted to the 1974 miners' strike by putting industry onto a three-day week to reduce energy consumption] — a new form of government by catastrophe — for which he was rewarded with defeat in the General Election. Nothing like this had ever been heard of before.[6]

The early 1970s saw a return to the pattern of national, official strikes seen in the early part of the twentieth century. In 1971 Upper Clyde Shipbuilders decided to sack 2,500 workers. The whole workforce, 8,500 of them, occupied the shipyard and 200,000 Scottish workers struck in solidarity. Some 80,000 of them demonstrated in support of the UCS occupation. The chief Constable of Strathclyde called the prime minister and told him that he could not be responsible for keeping the peace on Clydeside unless the government backed down. UCS was saved and a wave of 200 factory occupations followed the shipyard workers' lead.

Strikes were often official, but the rank and file were in the saddle. Shop stewards had cut their teeth in the years from 1965 to 1968 when 95 percent of strikes were unofficial and this power and confidence was now the driving force whether strikes were official or not.

The steward organisation at the north London engineering factory of ENV graphically shows the depth of this confidence. Stewards there got rid of one foreman after another, competing with one another about who could be the first to cause the foreman to have a nervous breakdown. This rank and file confidence also took organisational form. For example, in 1970 the Liaison Committee for the Defence of Trade Unions — a rank and file body coordinated by the Communist Party and its supporters — called

43

an unofficial one day strike against the Tory Industrial Relations Bill and 600,000 workers came out on strike. Besides this Committee were the London Docks Liaison Committee, the Building Workers Joint Strike Committee, the Exhibition Workers Committee, the London Sheet Metal Workers Organisation and others.

The 1972 miners' strike is another example of the rank and file in charge. Rank-and-file activists organized flying pickets which spread across the country to shut off the supply of coal to the power stations and to industry. They were able to draw on the support of their counterparts in other unions. It was this solidarity spreading through the grassroots which was decisive at the turning-point of the strike — the Battle of Saltley Gates. By the beginning of February 1972 the last substantial stockpile of coke was at Saltley depot in Birmingham. The police were under instructions from the Tory Home Secretary, Reginald Maudling, to keep Saltley open. Even 3,000 miners led by the young Arthur Scargill, who at that time was running the Barnsley miners' strike committee, couldn't shut it down. So the miners appealed to the trade unionists of Birmingham. Scargill addressed the East Birmingham District Committee of the Amalgamated Union of Engineering Workers. 'We don't want your pound notes,' he told them. 'Will you go down in history as the working class in Birmingham who stood by while the miners were battered down or will you become immortal? I do not ask you — I *demand* that you come out on strike.'[7]

The AUEW voted for strike action, and were followed by a number of other major unions. Scargill describes what happened on Thursday 10 February outside Saltley depot:

miners were tired, physically and mentally desperately weary. ... And then over this hill came a banner and I've never seen so many people following a banner. As far as the eye could see it was just a mass of people marching towards Saltley. There was a huge roar and from the other side of the hill they were coming the other way. ... there were five approaches to Saltley; it was in a hollow, they were arriving from every direction. And our lads were jumping in the air with emotion — a fantastic situation . . . I got hold of the megaphone and I started to chant through it: 'Close the Gates! Close the Gates!'and it was taken up, just like a football crowd. It was booming through Saltley: 'Close the Gates'. It reverberated right across the hollow and each time they shouted this slogan they moved and the police, who were four deep, couldn't help it, they were getting moved in. Capper, the Chief Constable of Birmingham, took a swift decision. He said 'Close the Gates' and they swung them to. Hats were in the air, you've never seen anything like it in your life. Absolute delirium on the part of the people there. Because the Birmingham working class had become involved — not as observers but as participants. The whole of the East District of the Birmingham AUEW were out on strike, 100,000 were out on strike, you know. It was tremendous. And they were still marching in from Coventry and other places, still advancing into Saltley. It was estimated that there were 20,000 in this area.[8]

Reginald Maudling, the Tory Home Secretary in 1972, wrote in his memoirs:

> The then Chief Constable of Birmingham assured me that only over his dead body would they [the pickets] . . . succeed [in closing Saltley]. I felt constrained to ring him the next day after it happened to enquire after his health! I am sure the decision he took was a wise one, because the number of strikers was so great, and feelings were running so high, that any attempt by the relatively small body of police who could be assembled to keep the depot open by force could have led to very grave consequences. Some of my colleagues asked me afterwards, why I had not sent in troops to support the police, and I remember asking them one single question: 'if they had been sent in, should they have gone in with their rifles loaded or unloaded?' Either course could have been disastrous.[9]

Douglas Hurd, later himself a Tory cabinet minister, then one of Heath's advisers, noted in his diary after Saltley: 'The government is now vainly wandering over the battlefield looking for someone to surrender to and being massacred all the time.'[10] The miners' demands were conceded. The Battle of Saltley Gates was a historic victory. It was a victory for rank-and-file militancy, not for the leadership of the miners union then dominated by the right wing under Joe Gormley.

The same was true of the other high-point of 1972, the release of the Pentonville Five. Dockworkers took unofficial action, against the wishes of the TGWU general secretary, the left winger

Jack Jones, to defend jobs against the spread of containerization. This brought them into conflict with the Tory Industrial Relations Act. As a result five docks shop stewards were gaoled on 21 July for defying the law. The dockers marched on Pentonville prison, where the five were being held, and called for strike action from other workers to free them. Their call was answered by Fleet Street printers, Sheffield engineers, Heathrow airport workers, London bus workers, and lorry drivers. The Amalgamated Union of Engineering Workers (AUEW) announced that it would hold a one-day strike. On 26 July the TUC General Council reluctantly decided to call a one-day General Strike. That same day, however an obscure government lawyer called the Official Solicitor persuaded the House of Lords to free the five. Workers' industrial power had humbled the law.

The miners' and dockers' victories created a climate of growing panic within the ruling class. Discussing the possibility of a General Strike in June 1972 the *Financial Times* commented: 'most of the leaders on both sides realize this kind of "simple" solution, far from clearing the air, might divide the nation more deeply than at any time since, perhaps 1688, and that whoever won, it might take generations to clear up the mess.'[11] During the winter of 1973-74 confidence drained away from the ruling class. Tony Benn describes in his diaries a dinner held for Labour leaders by the Confederation of British Industry at which the latter were 'utterly gloomy'. In December 1973 another leading businessmen told Benn 'we were heading for a slump and food riots and there must be a national government'.[12] At much the same time, one Tory cabinet minister, John Davies, was telling his family to enjoy their Christmas, as it might be their last together. The Heath government's final confrontation with the workers' movement came when the miners struck again in February 1974. The miners brought the government down, but its Labour successor came to the rescue of British capitalism.

The strength and militancy of rank-and-file organization in the early 1970s had not developed in a political vacuum. The Communist Party, still at that time an organization with over 20,000 members and considerable industrial influence, provided the political cement binding together militants in different unions and industries. Communist Party activists played a key role in sectors with a history of militancy — for example, in the South Wales, Scottish, and Yorkshire coalfields. Most figures on the left had been members of the CP, even if, like Scargill, they left it. Their political education came through the Party. Often at a local level coalitions of left-wing stewards, many of them Communists, would meet regularly to discuss politics and strategy and to co-ordinate action. This was true, for example, of the Barnsley Miners' Forum, founded by Scargill in 1967, and of the Manchester engineers' Broad Left, the power-base of Hugh Scanlon, who was elected AUEW president that same year.[13]

However, the main thrust of CP industrial strategy was not to build a national rank-and-file movement but to elect left-wing trade-union leaders. As early as 1945, when CP membership reached its peak of 55,000, its factory branches were disbanded. In 1951 a programme was adopted, *The British Road to Socialism*, which committed the CP to seeking change through parliament by helping to secure the election of a left-wing Labour government. In the unions this meant building the Broad Lefts as electoral coalitions designed to win official positions for Communists and their left-wing Labour allies. By the late 1960s this approach seemed to be gaining ground, above all with the election of Jones and Scanlon, the so called 'Terrible Twins' of the left, to head the two key industrial unions, the TGWU and the AUEW. But the price of this electoral strategy was the CP's growing reluctance to clash with the left officials. Thus the Liaison Committee for the Defence of Trade Unions, founded by the Party to resist anti-union legislation, led two large unofficial strikes against the Labour government's proposals in 1969, followed by two others in 1970-1, but made no serious effort to link together rank-and-file militants in the much greater struggles of 1972-74.

CHAPTER 5

Era of defeats: 1974-89

A Labour government was returned to office in March 1974, just as the world economy slipped into the first great slump since the 1930s. The fall of the Heath government and its pay policy was accompanied by an explosion of wage-struggles that were particularly significant since they often involved groups of workers not previously known for their militancy such as teachers, civil servants, and hospital workers. Harried by the financial markets, the Labour government sought desperately to restore the stability of British capitalism. In June 1975 it imposed strict wage-controls. These only held thanks to the support of the trade-union leaders, and in particular those 'Terrible Twins', Jones and Scanlon.

Under a Tory government workers' resistance was summed up by the simple phrase 'Tories out'. But such a simple approach could not be adopted once Labour came to power. Workers expected 'their' party to do things for them and, for a time at least, were willing to make sacrifices in the belief that Labour must be pursuing policies for a good reason and to benefit workers. When Labour began to introduce anti working class policies therefore there was disorientation throughout the labour movement and no clear idea of how to resist them. Under the Social Contract the TUC had agreed with the government the TUC set out to restrain the wage-militancy that had brought down Heath. In the short term it was successful. Strikes and real wages collapsed, while mass unemployment soared.

There were also longer-term qualitative changes on the shop

floor that made the union leaders' task easier.[1] The stewards' most basic function, that of negotiating the rate of pay for the job, was taken away from them. Instead of national negotiation for basic wages and then negotiation factory by factory or even shop by shop for extras — piece rates, bonuses and the like — as had been the norm through much of the 1960s and 1970s, Measured Day Work was introduced. For example, this meant that all workers in similar grades working for, say, Leyland Cars would get the same wage rates and there was now no way of getting extras in individual factories, let alone individual shops. Meanwhile, the number of full-time convenors and senior stewards increased rapidly until by the late 1970s there were over 7,000 of them, two or three times the number of full-time officials. The effect was to extend the trade-union bureaucracy down into the workplace, creating within shopfloor organization a layer of stewards isolated from the workers they represented.

Secondly, Jones's and Scanlon's betrayals represented the collapse of the strategy of creating Broad Lefts to win control of unions in which most politically aware militants had placed their hopes in the late 1960s and early 1970s. The CP moved steadily to the right till by the end of the 1970s a faction emerged around the magazine *Marxism Today*, edited by Martin Jacques (now deputy editor of the *Independent*), increasingly open in its hostility to the very idea of class politics. This political degeneration was accompanied by a steady erosion of the CP's working-class base. Militants were thus deprived of their main organizational framework.

Thirdly, throughout the struggles of the preceding period the politics of the shop stewards had been of left-wing reformism at best. The acute economic crisis of the mid-1970s meant that this would no longer do. During the long economic boom workers had been able to screw higher wages out of the bosses while continuing to believe that, for example, their prosperity depended on the profitability of the company for which they worked. But what should they do when profits were falling and their workmates were being laid off?

Many leading stewards came to the conclusion that — just as Scanlon and Jones were helping the Labour government prop up British capitalism — they should do their bit to keep their own company going, even if this meant accepting cuts in wages and conditions. Thus Derek Robinson, a CP member and convenor of

49

the British Leyland plant at Longbridge in Birmingham, in 1977 played a decisive part in preventing a rebellion by toolroom workers against Labour's pay policy turning into an all-out strike.[2] A month later, when electricians in Port Talbot steel works went on strike, the rest of the workers there were told to cross the picket line, breaking the strike. In April that year, 5,000 AEU members struck in Heathrow, but 54,000 other workers were told to cross the picket lines and the strike went down.

The labour movement was thus undergoing a threefold crisis, of organization, ideology, and leadership.[3] There were those who sought to swim against the stream. The International Socialists, predecessor of the Socialist Workers Party, grew rapidly during the struggles of the early 1970s. In particular, it was able to recruit a significant layer of shop stewards dissatisfied with the increasing caution of the CP and the trade-union lefts. By September 1974 IS had some 4,000 members and 40 factory branches. This expanding industrial influence was built by IS members establishing a number of rank-and-file papers which aimed to group together militants on the basis of existing shop stewards' organization, or, in sectors such as hospitals, to start to construct such organization. (Table 2).

Table 2 Rank and File papers, March 1973

Carworker	9	*6,000*	*45%*
Collier	6	*5,000*	*33%*
Hospital worker	7	*6,000*	*60%*
Platform (bus workers)	3	*3,000*	*50%*
Textile worker	1	*1,500*	*nil*
Case Con (social workers)	4	*5000*	*95%*
Journalists Charter	4	*2,000*	*60%*
NALGO Action News	8	*6,000*	*98%*
Rank and File teacher	13	*10,000*	*42%*
Redder Tape	4	*3,000*	*57%*
Scots Rank and File	3	*2,000*	*15%*
Tech Teacher	4	*2,000*	*30%*
Dock Worker	12	*5,000*	*99%*
GEC Rank and File	5	*8,000*	*60%*
Building Worker	6	*2,0000*	*27%*
Electricians Special	3	*2.000*	*15%*

In March 1974 IS took the first step in initiating a national rank-and-file movement that would link together militants in different industries and operate, unlike the CP and the Broad Lefts, independently of the officials. A National Rank-and-File Organizing Committee was set up and three delegate conferences were held, two in 1974 and one in 1977. The last was attended by 522 delegates from 251 trade-union bodies, a perfectly respectable level of support. But the entire initiative was still-born.

In part this was a consequence of the fact that IS's industrial base was still at this time far narrower than the CP's and indeed was rapidly weakened by a wave of victimizations in 1973-74, which caused the collapse of several key factory branches in the car plants. More fundamental, however, was that IS's rank-and-file initiative was launched just as the pendulum of class struggle began to swing back in the bosses' favour. The erosion of shop-floor organization deprived the potential IS rank-and-file movement of its base. By the early 1980s the surviving rank-and-file caucuses in different unions had degenerated into electoral coalitions little different from the Broad Lefts and the SWP decided to wind them up. The failure of this attempt to build a national rank-and-file movement was one small symptom of a substantial shift in the balance of class forces in capital's favour which took place under the 1974-79 Labour government. This shift did not mean that strikes or industrial militancy came to an end. Though Scanlon and Jones were able to hold the line and crush a rebellion against Labour's pay policy in 1977, the dam broke towards the end of 1978. The 'Winter of Discontent' — a wave of strikes involving Ford workers, lorry drivers, and a wide range of public-sector employees — finally smashed the Social Contract. The Labour government staggered on for a few more months before going down to electoral defeat in May 1979.

The aim of the new Tory government under Margaret Thatcher was to reverse the defeats the ruling class had suffered at workers' hands in the early 1970s. Thatcher proceeded cautiously at first, pursuing a strategy of isolating and defeating key groups of workers one by one and introducing anti-union legislation gradually and piecemeal. The strategy — based on a report drawn up by Nicholas Ridley in 1978, when the Tories were still in opposition — led to a series of confrontations: with the steelworkers in 1980, the health-workers in 1982, the miners in 1984-85, the News International printers in 1985-86 and the dockers in 1989. [4]

The ruling class won all these battles, though they were often hard-fought. The steelworkers, a previously conservative group of workers, built a formidable mass-picketing organization during their first national strike since 1926. And the men and women of the mining communities wrote an epic page in the history of the British labour movement during their heroic year-long strike of 1984-85. There were moments during that dispute — above all, when mass pickets sought twice to block the supply of coke from the Orgreave plant near Sheffield, and when scabbing briefly provoked a national docks strike in July 1984 — when the miners were on the verge of winning. Walter Marshall, boss of the Central Electricity Generating Board during the strike later admitted that coal stocks at the power stations were running dangerously low in autumn of 1984.

The Tory government massively mobilized the police to defeat the pickets. But that was not the decisive factor in the strike's defeat. The Area leaderships of the NUM blocked effective mass picketing and threw away the potential that existed, above all at Orgreave, to repeat the great victory at Saltley. Scargill, no longer a rank-and-file activist but, since 1981, NUM president, proved to be a prisoner of a union machine unwilling to adopt the tactics needed to win the strike. And the leaders of the TUC and the Labour Party earned for themselves an ignominy comparable to that of their predecessors in 1926 by leaving the miners to fight alone.[5] The same pattern was repeated in the other great battles of the period. Again and again the trade-union bureaucracy, even when goaded into action, refused to prosecute the fight with the same ruthlessness and determination that the Tories showed.

However, there was more to the defeats of the 1980s than this. The victories of the early 1970s were won by the rank and file despite the union leaders. But these rank-and-file organisations were severely weakened during the Social Contract years of the Labour government of 1974-79. Thus the miners' branch and lodge officers had increasingly become full-timers, while the different Areas of the union had become divided from one another by a pit incentive scheme forced through in 1977 by the then Labour Energy Secretary, Tony Benn. These divisions were a crucial factor behind the decision of most Nottinghamshire miners — who received higher payments than most other miners thanks to Benn's incentive scheme — to scab on the 1984-85 strike.

The weakening of shop stewards' organization meant that it was much harder to win solidarity from other groups of workers. Scargill pointed out that in 1972 'the [miners'] picket line didn't close Saltley, . . . the working class closed Saltley.' The mass pickets at Orgreave took place, like the Battle of Saltley Gates near a large concentration of engineering workers with a history of militancy and left-wing politics, in Sheffield. But this time there were no strikes by engineers, no flood of marchers to join the picket-line. Battered by closures and redundancies, the Sheffield engineering workers kept their heads down. As Tony Cliff put it, 'workers who lack the confidence to stand up to their own bosses cannot be expected to come out in support of other workers.'[6]

The balance of power had shifted not just from labour to capital, but from the rank and file to the trade-union bureaucracy. The full-time officials, no longer under pressure from a self-confident shopfloor, presided over defeat after defeat. The TUC could confidently propagate their 'new realism', according to which strikes were a thing of the past and support the efforts of Neil Kinnock to drive the Labour party to the right. Particularly after the defeat of the miners' strike, militant trade unionism was written off as a thing of the past. But is it?

CHAPTER 6

Tasks for today

The British working-class movement in the mid-1990s is in a transitional situation. All the signs are that the great downturn in the class struggle of the late 1970s and the 1980s is over. Workplace trade-union organization has emerged from this era of defeat weakened, but enormously resilient, as the first chapter of this book demonstrated. There are still some 300,000 shop stewards and workplace representatives, even if the connection between them and the workers they represent is often not as close as it was in the 1960s and early 1970s. At the same time, workers are still not confident enough to go on the offensive against the bosses. One of the clearest indicators of this is the tight control full-time officials continue to exert.

A number of disputes in the last few years show how the nature of class struggle is beginning to change. Take the signal workers strike of late 1994. Firstly, the strike was almost completely solid, despite the best efforts of the government and the employers. Out of 4,600 signal workers only 70 scabbed. Another 400 signal workers joined the union during the strike and the strike won an 8.7 percent pay rise, a reduction in the working week and longer holidays. This is a very different picture to the train drivers' strike of 1982 which collapsed in ignominious failure after only a few hours. However, the 1994 strike remained wholly in the control of the union bureaucracy — other rail workers were never asked to strike and calls to make the strike all out, rather than a programme of one and two day strikes, were easily brushed aside.

In the wake of the signal workers strike, Rover workers were offered 10 percent over two years. The union officials managed to sell it to their members, but only with the tiniest of majorities — 51 percent.

But against these signs of revival we have to set the TGWU leadership's agreement that local government workers will only get a rise of just over 1.5 percent plus £100 in 1994-95 and 1.4 percent plus £100 in 1995-96. When we look at unofficial action its the same mixed picture — one step forward, two steps back.

The good news is that the unofficial strike is back. Time and again there have been unofficial strikes in, for example, the Post Office over the last few years. In November 1990 700 Oxford postal workers, 85 percent of them men, struck unofficially and illegally over the harassment of a black woman cleaner by a supervisor. Offices in Abingdon, Wallingford, Kidlington, Cowley, Headlington, Northampton and Swindon took solidarity action. In 1994 action by a few hundred postal workers in Milton Keynes drew solidarity strikes from 30,000 postal workers around the country. The same year a Liverpool postal worker kept his job, despite having hit a foreman who ridiculed his speech impediment, when 2,000 of his fellow workers struck in his support. And in early 1995 almost the entire London postal area was strike bound when the victimisation of 150 postal workers in North West London led to unofficial and illegal secondary action. Elsewhere, Sefton council workers managed to fend off both the courts and the union leaders in a successful unofficial strike against the privatisation of council services.

But there is bad news too. Many of the unofficial strikes are short lived because the workers involved do not have sufficient organisation or confidence to resist the union bureaucracy when it intervenes to enforce a deal, even when that deal is very poor indeed. And the overall level of unofficial action is still low, perhaps 5 percent of the total. So, although the revival is real enough, it is still not powerful enough to change the overall pattern of struggle.

This situation is unlikely to continue indefinitely. Experience teaches us that, sooner or later, the resentments that have accumulated during the long years of defeat will burst out in an explosion of struggles. The example of the mid-1930s suggests that there is more than one way in which a new upturn can develop. It may as in the US and Britain, be a consequence chiefly of economic factors — of a fall in the level of unemployment which gives workers a sense of their greater bargaining power and more confidence. Or, as in the case of France in 1968, it may be a political crisis which gives workers the confidence to struggle. The general political crisis experienced by all the major west European states in the 1990s may well be creating the conditions for such an explosion.[1]

Any upturn will breathe new life into shop stewards' organization. Shop stewards cannot escape from the general contradiction involved in trade unionism — that of seeking to organize resistance to exploitation within the limits of capitalism, from which arises the liability of even the most militant workers to sectionalism and reformism. They have always been under pressure to act as 'managers of discontent' who seek to control the rank and file and even to discipline them. Discussing their support for management's efforts to force up productivity in the 1980s and early 1990s, a convenor at a Rover car plant admitted:

> We have co-operated with management because we want Rover to succeed. But this has opened up a rift between us [the senior convenors] and the shop floor, who regard us as being in league with management.[2]

Nevertheless, despite the development of the full-time convenors, shop stewards' organization remains qualitatively different from official union structures in its potential responsiveness to rank-and-file pressures. Even full-time stewards are normally subject to regular elections. They are liable to victimization by management and will lose their jobs if their plants are closed. Derek Robinson, the Communist convenor at Longbridge, played a crucial role in containing shopfloor discontent under the 1974-79 Labour government. Once the Tories had taken office he was sacked by the new hard-nosed management of Michael Edwards.

The great mass of shop stewards and other lay union representatives enjoy no real privileges. On the contrary, they have to hold together workplace union organization, often in very difficult conditions. They will play a vital role in any large scale revival in workers' struggles.

Even the most corrupt and decayed workplace organization can be recaptured by the rank and file with comparative ease. In all probability, the new workers' militancy will often involve the rank and file confronting or even by-passing existing shop-steward structures. But the long-term effect will be to renew these structures. Experience suggests that socialist political activists will play an indispensable part in rebuilding rank-and-file organization. Richard Croucher in his study of engineering workers in the 1930s and 1940s stresses how vital a role was played by Communist Party activists in the shop stewards' movement then:

> The Communist shop stewards of the 1930s . . . became extremely important in the factory trade-movement, becoming convenors, senior stewards and so on. This was partly because they had proved so effective in building the shop-steward system in the first place: they had been prepared to go where wiser men feared to tread and had reaped the reward. It was also because the shop-steward system was completely 'open' . . . In many factories those who wanted the [convenor's] job could have it. The left wingers did not 'infiltrate' the shop-floor organization; rather, they grew with it, at its head.[3]

In the US at much the same time, a tiny Trotskyist group, the Communist League, was able to play a leading role in the mass strikes waged by Minneapolis teamsters in 1934 — one of the key struggles which paved the way for the great wave of unionization in the US in 1936-37.[4]

The rank-and-file movements which emerge from the struggles of the 1990s will not be identical to their predecessors. The working class has changed over the past generation. Some industries have declined while others have expanded. Women play a far more important part as wage-earners than they did in the past. But certain fundamental lessons from the past still apply, one of the most important of these concerns the role of socialist organization. Experience shows that national rank-and-file movements can only be built on the initiative of revolutionary socialists. The actual programmes of these movements may consist chiefly of straightforward trade-union demands. Moreover, to succeed they have to unite workers of all political views in support of these demands. But their leadership has to come from revolutionaries. Only revolutionaries can provide the clear sighted opposition to the bosses and the necessary degree of independence from the state and the trade union leaders. Even left-wing reformists have a proven record of looking to the state and seeking compromises with trade union leaders and the ruling class.[5]

The problems involved in building a national rank-and file movement are questions for the future, when basic shop stewards' organization has been renewed, strengthened, and extended by workers' struggles. What can socialists do now, to begin to lay the basis for this? There are four key things to remember.

Build strong sectional organization.

The basis of all effective trade-union organization lies in its roots in the workplace. Shop stewards' organization was at its strongest in the 1950s and 1960s because in well-unionized factories workers in each individual section had the confidence and solidarity to act together. It was on this that the power of the shop stewards rested.

The erosion of piecework in the late 1960s and 1970s undermined this sectional strength. Ironically the attacks mounted on national agreements by the Tories and the employers in recent years may be beginning to create conditions in which sectional strength can be rebuilt. The government's own New Earnings Survey found in September 1994 that many pay settlements in both the public and the private sectors were running well above the 1.5 per cent limit imposed by the Tory chancellor Kenneth Clarke. The *Financial Times* reported 'that an increasing amount of wage bargaining is carried out at local level' and that 'there is an enormous amount of wage drift in the economy'.[6]

Wage drift is a symptom of workers' greater bargaining power. Socialists at work should be in the forefront of those seeking to use this power to build strong organization.

Solidarity

Sectional organization on its own can degenerate into sectionalism, into ignoring the plight of other workers. One of the main elements of the developing downturn in the mid-1970s was the weakening of solidarity between different groups of workers. The trade-union bureaucracy bears a heavy responsibility for this. Twice in the early spring of 1977 workers were instructed by their leaders to cross picket-lines, during a strike by electricians at Port Talbot steelworks and then when maintenance engineers at Heathrow came out. The Tories sought to re-enforce this trend by making secondary action — picketing of other workers not directly involved in a dispute — illegal. This gave the TUC another excuse to let the miners fight alone in the Great Strike of 1984-85.[7]

None of this means that workers' solidarity died in the 1980s. On the contrary, the Great Miners' Strike received very strong support from a substantial minority of the population. As the strike went on, a dense network of miners' support groups spread across the country collecting money and goods to help keep the people of the mining communities going. Twinning arrangements linked together particular trade-union branches and miners' villages.[8] The level of solidarity shown with the signalworkers in their dispute of 1994, both by the general public and by organised workers, was also very impressive. This made it very easy to collect money for the signal workers, though the decline of the Labour left meant that this was chiefly done by the SWP and its supporters.

Socialists need to constantly strengthen traditions of solidarity. By collecting money for workers on strike, and by taking strikers' delegations around other workplaces and union branches they can help re-establish the connections between different groups of workers. Solidarity isn't just developed through support given to industrial disputes. Broader political issues can be just as important in developing the habit of solidarity. The Spanish Civil War of 1936-39 was a key issue for the left then. Tens of thousands of working class socialists rallied to the Republican cause and many of them — for example from the South Wales coalfield — volunteered to serve with the International Brigades in Spain. Today, issues like support for the Anti Nazi League or the Coalition Against the Criminal Justice Act are vital in making the workers in a particular section feel that they are not alone, but part of a great movement which hates the bosses, the Tories and the right wing.

Work with and against the officials.

Trade unions are the mass defence organizations of the working class. It is a central theme of the Marxist tradition that socialists should be actively involved in them, fighting side by side with their fellow-workers. In this way they can show in practice that revolutionary ideas offer the best way for the working class to pursue its interests. It is an inevitable consequence of their activity as trade unionists that socialists will find themselves standing for, and often being elected as shop stewards and other kinds of lay union representatives. Some involvement in the official machine will be unavoidable. Particularly in conditions where the trade-union bureaucracy still has the initiative, socialists will have to adopt a careful approach. They should constantly press for official action and support it when it takes place. At the same time they must warn their fellow workers not to rely on the full-time officials and do everything possible to develop the ability and confidence of the rank and file to fight independently of the officials.

Official action shouldn't be seen as a barrier to what trade union militants are pressing for. On the contrary, when the officials do move it gives an additional authority to activists' demands. Socialists should build on official action arguing, where necessary, that it should go further and using it to develop a stronger and more self reliant rank and file.

Socialists' aim in the workplaces is to create the kind of rank-and-file organization that can take as its watchword the Clyde Workers' Committee's great declaration in 1915: 'We will support the officials just so long as they rightly represent the workers, but we will act immediately they misrepresent them.'

The role of socialist politics

Trade unionism, however militant, however controlled from below, is not enough. The experience of the 1970s and 1980s shows how even the best rank-and-file organization is vulnerable to the ups and downs of the capitalist economy. As long as capitalism exists, workers can expect at best to limit their exploitation, not to do away with it. Only a socialist revolution through which workers take power away from the capitalist class and begin to rebuild society on the basis of their own democratic mass organizations offers an escape from the endless to and fro, the ceaseless succession of advances and retreats, which is the fate of the labour movement under capitalism. But that requires political organization, a party.

Revolutionary socialist organization is a crucial to building workplace union organization. It can, as the Communist Party did between the 1930s and the early 1970s, create a politically organized community of militants in different unions and industries. The Socialist Workers Party today is seeking, by developing a network of its supporters in the workplaces, to lay the basis for recreating such a community. In this way, the framework can be built on which a new national rank-and-file movement can grow.

But the aim of a socialist party isn't simply to bring trade-union militants together. It is to help them widen their horizons and see how their own particular situation, and the battles in which they engage are part of the much broader struggle to rid the world of the monster of capitalism. As Marx argued nearly 150 years ago, the logic of the struggle of the working class within capitalism is to develop into a movement that liberates humankind once and for all from class exploitation and all its horrors.

Useful addresses

TUC Affiliated Trade Unions

AEEU
Amalgamated Engineering and Electrical Union
Hayes Court, West Common Road
Bromley, Kent
0181 462 7755

AMU
Associated Metalworkers Union
92 Worsley Road North
Worsley, Manchester
01204 793245

ASLEF
Associated Society of Locomotive Engineers and Firemen
9 Arkwright Road
London NW3
0171 431 0275

FDA
Association of First Division Civil Servants
2 Caxton Street
London SW1
0171 222 6242

AUT
Association of University Teachers
United House, 9 Pembridge Road
London W11
0171 221 4370

BFAWU
Bakers, Food and Allied Workers Union
Stanborough House, Great North Road
Stanborough, Welwyn Garden City
01707 260150

BIFU
Banking, Insurance and Finance Union
Sheffield House, 1b Amity Grove
London SW20
0181 946 9151

EQUITY
British Actors Equity Association
Guild House, Upper St Martins Lane
London WC2
0171 370 6000

BALPA
British Airline Pilots Association
81 New Road, Harlington, Hayes, Middlesex
0181 476 4000

BECTU
Broadcasting, Entertainment, Cinematograph and Theatre Union
111 Wardour Street, London W1
0171 437 8506

CWU
Communication Workers Union
c/o UCW House, Crescent Lane
London SW4
0171 622 9977

CSMTS
Card Setting Machine Tenters Society
48 Scar End Lane, Staincliffe
Dewsbury, West Yorkshire
01924 400206

CATU
Ceramic and Allied Trades Union
Hillcrest House, Garth STreet
Hanley, Stoke on Trent
01782 272755

CSP
Chartered Society of Physiotherapy
14 Bedford Row
London WC1
0171 242 1941

CPSA
Civil and Public Servicies Association
160 Falcon Road
London SW11
0171 9244 2727

EIS
Educational Institute of Scotland
46 Moray Place
Edinburgh EH3
0131 225 6244

EPIU
Electrical and Plumbing Industries Union
Park House, 64 Wandswoth Common
North Side
London SW 18
0181 874 04558

EFTU
Engineering and Fastener Trade Union
42 Galton Road, Warley
West Midlands
0121 429 2594

EMA
Engineers and Managers Association
Flaxman House, Gogmore Lane
Chertsey, Surrey
01932 577077

FAA
Film Artistes Association
61 Marloes Road, London W8
0171 937 4567

FBU
Fire Brigades Union
Bradley House, 68 Coombe Road
Kingston upon Thames, Surrey
0181 541 1765

GMB
General and Municipal Boilermakers Union
22/24 Worple Road
London SW19
0181 947 3131

GUALO
General Union of Associations of Loom Overloockers
9 Wellington Street, St John's
Blackburn
01254 51760

GPMU
Graphical, Paper and Media Union
Keys House, 63/67 Bromham Road
Bedford
01234 351521

HCSA
Hospital Consultants and Specialists Association
1 Kingsclere Road, Overton
Basingstoke, Hampshire
01256 771777

IRSF
Inland Revenue Staff Federation
Douglas Houghton House
231 Vauxhall Bridge Road
London SW1
0171 834 8254

ISTC
Iron and Steel Trades Confederation
Swinton House, 324 Grays Inn Road
London WC1
0171 837 6691

MSF
Manufacturing Science Finance
Park House 64/66 Wandsworth Common
North Side
London SW18
0181 871 2100

MU
Musicians Union
60/62 Clapham Road
London SW9
0171 582 5566

NACODS
National Association of Colliery Overmen, Deputies and Shotfirers
Simpson House, 48 Nether Hall Road
Doncaster, South Yorkshire
01302 368015

NACO
National Association of Cooperative Officials
Coronation House, Arndale Centre
Manchester M4
0161 834 6029

NALHM
National Association of Licensed House Managers
9 Coombe Lane, Raynes Park
London SW20

NAPO
National Association of Probation Officers
3/3 Chivalry Road
London SW11
0171 223 4887

NASUWT
National Association of Schoolmasters Union of Women Teachers
5 King Street
London WC2
0o171 379 9499

NATFHE
The University and College Lecturers Union
27 Britannia Street
London WC1
0171 837 3636

NLBD
National League of the Blind and Disabled
2 Tenterden Road
London N17
0181 808 6030

NUCPS
National Union of Civil and Public Servants
New Bridgewater House
5-13 Grate Suffold Street
London SE1
0171 928 9671

NUDAGO
National Union of Domestic Appliances and General Operatives
7/8 Imperial Buildings
Corporation Street, Rotherham
South Yorkshire
01709 382820

NUIW
National Union of Insurance Workers
27 Old Gloucester Street
London WC1
0171 405 6798

NUJ
National Union of Journalists
Acorn House, 314/320 Grays Inn Road
London WC1
0171 278 7916

NUKFAT
National Union of Knitwear, Footwear and Apparel Trades
55 New Walk
Leicester
0116 255 6703

NULMW
National Union of Lock and Metal Workers
Bellamy House, Wilkes Street Willenhall
West Midlands
01902 366651

NUMAST
National Union of Maritime, Aviation and Shipping Transport Officers
Oceanaire House, 750/760 High road
London E11
0181 9896677

NUM
National Union of Mineworkers
Miners Offices, 2 Huddersfield Road
Barnsley, South Yorkshire
01226 284006

RMT
National Union of Rail, Maritime and Transport Workers
Unity House, 205 Euston Road, London NW1
0171 387 4771

NUT
National Union of Teachers
Hamilton House, Mabledon Place, London WC1
0171 3886191

PLCWTWU
Power Loom Carpet Weavers and Textile Workers Union
148 Hurcott Road, Kidderminster
Worcestershire
01562 823192

POA
Prison Officers Association
Cronin House, 245 Church Street
London N9
0181 803 0255

RUBSSO
Rossendale Union of Boot, Shoe and Slipper Operatives
7 Tenterfield Street, Waterfoot
 Rossendale, Lancashire
01706 215657

SOR
Society of Radiographers
14 Upper Wimpole Street
London W1
0171 935 5726

STE
Society of Telecom Executives
1 Park Road, Teddington
Middlesex
0181 943 5181

TGWU
Transport and General Workers Union
Transport House, Palace Street, Victoria
London SW1
0171 828 7788

TSSA
Transport Salaried Staffs Association
Walkden House, 10 Melton Street
London NW1
0101 387 2101

UCATT
Union of Construction, Allied Trades and Technicians
UCATT House, 177 Abbeville Road, London SW4
0171 622 2442

USDAW
Union of Shop, Distributive and Allied Workers
Oakley, 188 Wilmslow Road, Fallowfield
Manchester M14
0161 224 2804

UTW
Union of Textile Workers
Foxlowe, Market Place, Leek
Staffordshire
01538 382068

UNISON
Local Government and Health Workers Union
Unison Centre, Holborn Tower
137 High Holborn
London WC1
0171 404 1884
(UNISON were set to move at the end of March 1995)

URTU
United Road Transport Union
76 High Lane, Chorlton cum Hardy
Manchester M21
0161 881 6245

WGGB
Writers Guild of Great Britain
430 Edgeware Road
London W2
0171 723 8074

Campaigns and other organizations

Anti Nazi League
PO Box 2566
London N4
0171 924 0313

Asylum Rights Campaign
The Refugee Council, 3 Bondway
London SW18
0171 582 6922

British Safety Council
70 Chancellors Road
London W6
0181 741 1231

Child Poverty Action Group
1-5 Bath Street
London EC1
0171 253 3406

Coalition Against the Criminal Justice Act
PO Box 6786
London N17 9NY
0181 801 5285

Construction Safety Campaign
225 Poplar high Street
London E14
0171 537 7220

Disability Alliance
25 Denmark Street
London WC2
0171 379 6142

Equal Opportunities Commission
Overseas House, Quay Street
Manchester M3
0161 833 9244

Homeless Action
52-54 Featherstone Street
London EC1
0171 251 6783

Incomes Data Services
193 St John Street
London EC1
0171 250 3434

Industrial Relations Research Unit
University of Warwick
Coventry, West Midlands
0202 523523

Institute of Employment Rights
112 Greyhound Lane
Streatham
london SW16
0181 677 9644

Labour Research Department
78 Blackfriars Road
London SE1
0171928 3649

Low Pay Unit
27-29 Anwell Street
London EC1
0171 713 7616

National Abortion Campaign
Wesley House, 4 Wild Court
London WC2
0171 405 4801

National Association of Citizens Advice Bureaux
115-123 Pentonville Road
London N1
0171 833 2181

Shelter
88 Old Street
London EC1
0171 253 0202

Socialist Workers Party
PO Box 82
London E3 3LH
0171 538 5821

Socialist Worker Newspaper
PO Box 82
London E3 3LH
0171 538 0828

Society of Labour Lawyers
4 Kings Bench Walk, The Temple
London EC4
0171 353 0478

Terrance Higgins Trust
52-54 Grays Inn Road
London WC1
0171 831 0330

Trade Union Resource Centre
70 Lionel Street
Birmingham B3
0121 236 8323

Unemployment Unit
409 Brixton Road
London SW9
0171 737 8001

Workers Education Association
Temple House, 17 Victoria Park Square
London E2
0181 983 1515

Notes

Chapter 1

1. Quoted in R. Taylor, *The Future of the Unions*, (London 1994), p. 1.
2. D. Bird and L. Corcoran, 'Trade Union Membership and Density 1992-93', *Employment Gazette*, June 1994, Tables 6 and 7. See also 'Lies, Damned Lies and Union Density', *Labour Research* June 1994.
3. 'Collective Bargaining: Has it a Future?' *IDS Focus* 62, 1992 pp. 5-6.
4. 'Why White Collar Staff Join Trade Unions', *IRS Employment Trends* 565, August 1994.
5. Bird and Corcoran, 'Trade Union Membership', Table 7.
6. *1994 Survey of Industrial Action Trends*, Employment Law Department, Dibb Lupton Broomhead solicitors, London.

Chapter 2

1. L.D. Trotsky, *The Struggle Against Fascism in Germany*, (New York 1971), p. 158.
2. S. and B. Webb, *The History of Trade Unionism 1666-1920*, (Edinburgh 1919), p. 204.
3. R. Michels *Political Parties*, (Glencoe IL 1949), p. 19.
4. See J. Hinton and R. Hyman, *Trade Unions and Revolution*, (London 1975), pp. 18ff
5. On the wartime watershed see P. Addison, *The Road to 1945*, (London 1977).
6. *Rosa Luxemburg Speaks*, (New York 1970), pp. 214-17.

7. It is important not to confuse the Marxist theory of the trade union bureaucracy with the apparently closely related idea of the labour aristocracy. The latter phrase came into use among socialists in Britain in the mid nineteenth century to refer to the relatively small group of well paid craft workers then organized in trade unions. Compared to the mass of low paid, unskilled, and unorganized workers (many of them women and Irish immigrants), these certainly seemed like a privileged elite. Lenin took the idea much further during the First World War. He argued that the failure of the European labour movement to oppose the war reflected the fact that a substantial group of workers had in effect been bought off with the 'super-profits' the capitalists had been able to gain by exploiting the workers and peasants in the colonial empires. Even in straightforward economic terms this theory doesn't really stand up, since it is very hard to identify any particular group of Western workers who might have benefited from imperialism more than any others. Moreover, it was the group usually seen as the heart of the nineteenth century labour aristocracy — skilled metalworkers — who were in the vanguard of the great revolutionary upsurge of the European working class which swept the continent at the end of the First World War, from Petrograd and Moscow to Berlin, Turin, Sheffield and Glasgow. These traditionally well paid and organized workers were in the firing line because the wages and conditions they had achieved during the years of peaceful expansion were now under attack. In the struggles that developed stark divisions opened up between rank and file militancy and the conservatism of the bureaucracy even within old craft unions like the Amalgamated Society of Engineers. See T. Cliff, 'The Economic Roots of Reformism', in *Neither Washington nor Moscow*, (London, 1982), and T. Cliff and D. Gluckstein, *Marxism and the Trade Union Struggle*, (London, 1986), ch. 3.

8. J. Kelly and E. Heery, *Working for the Union*, (Cambridge, 1994), p. 65.

9. *Financial Times,* 17 September, 1994.

10. J. Baskin, *Striking Back*, (Johannesburg 1991), p. 461.

11. Kelly and Heery, *Working*, pp. 85-86.

12. See *Rosa Luxemburg Speaks*

13. 'Management and Law', *IDS Focus* 62, March 1992, p. 5.

14. See A. Callinicos and M. Simons, *The Great Strike*, (London 1985).

15. See M. Simons, 'A Battle Undermined', *Socialist Review,* December 1993 and A. Scargill's History Distorted, ibid., February 1994.
16. See T. Cliff and D. Gluckstein, *The Labour Party: A Marxist History*, (London 1988).
17. T. Cliff, 'On perspectives', *International Socialism* 35 (1969).
18. See C. Rosenburg, *1919*, (London 1987).
19. A. Bevan, *In Place of Fear*, (London 1952), pp. 20-1.
20. Quoted in Cliff and Gluckstein, *Marxism and the Trade Union Struggle*, p. 181.

Chapter 3

1. J. Hinton, *The First Shop Stewards Movement*, (London 1973), p. 80.
2. *Leon Trotsky on China*, (New York 1976), pp. 319-20.
3. A Gramsci, *Selections from the Political Writings 1910-1920*, (London 1977), pp. 65, 66.
4. The struggles and movements of the 1910s and 1920s have been explored in great depth in T. Cliff and D. Gluckstein, *Marxism and the Trade Unions Struggle* (London, 1986), and M. Woodhouse and B. Pearce, *Essays in the History of Communism in Britain*, (London, 1975).
5. R. Holton, *British Syndicalism 1900-1914*, (London 1976), p. 73.
6. Ibid., pp. 73, 99-100.
7. See Hinton, *First Shop Stewards Movement*.
8. Ibid., p. 296.
9. Quoted ibid., p. 308.
10. J. Degras, ed., *The Communist International 1919-1943 Documents*, (3 volumes, London 1956), I, p. 248.
11. J. Hinton and R. Hyman, *Trade Unions and Revolution*, pp. 14-15.
12. Quoted ibid,. p. 14.
13. Quoted R. Martin *Communism and the British Trade Unions 1924-33*. ((Oxford 1969), p.28.
14. Quoted Woodhouse and Pearce, *Essays*, p. 82.
15. Quoted Cliff and Gluckstein, *Marxism and the Trade Union Struggle*, p. 115.
16. Quoted, ibid., p. 117. Cliff and Gluckstein document in detail the Minority Movement's orientation on the left officials.

17. Quoted ibid., p. 129. See ibid., parts two and three on the General Strike.

18. Quoted Hinton and Hyman, *Trade Unions*. p. 34.

19. Quoted Cliff and Gluckstein *Marxism and the Trade Union Struggle*, pp. 246-7.

20. R. Hyman, *Strikes*, pp. 26-7.

21. See B.W.E. Alford, *Depression or Recovery?*, (London 1972)

22. R. Croucher, *Engineers at War*, (London 1982), p. 25.

23. Ibid., pp. 28-9.

24. Ibid., pp. 45,47.

25. Ibid., p. 40.

26. Ibid., p. 40-1, 112-13.

27. B. Darke, *The Communist Technique in Britain*, (London 1953), pp. 36, 38.

28. Ibid., pp. 20-1.

29. Croucher, *Engineers*, chs, 3,4,6.

Chapter 4

1. R. Hyman, *Strikes,* p. 45.

2. See T. Cliff and C. Barker, *Incomes Policy, Legislation and Shop Stewards*, (London 1966) pp. 105, 135

3. See C. Harman, *The Fire Last Time*, (London 1988), ch. 12.

4. See C. Harman, *Explaining the Crisis*, (London 1984).

5. R. Harrison, editor's introduction to *The Independent Collier*, (Hassocks 1978), pp. 2,1.

6. M. Crick, *Scargill and the Miners*, (Harmondsworth 1985).

7. A. Scargill, 'The New Unionism', *New Left Review* 92, (1975), pp. 18-19.

8. R. Maudling, *Memoirs*, ((London 19978), pp. 160-1.

9 . D. Hurd, *An End to Promises*, (London 1979), p. 103.

10. Quoted, A. Barnett, 'Class Struggle and the Heath Government', *New Left Review* 77, (1973), p. 14.

11. T. Benn, *Against the Tide*, (London 1990), pp. 70, 76.

12. On the Manchester Broad Left see J. Tocher, 'The Desire for Change', *Socialist Review*, September 1978.

Chapter 5

1. See T. Cliff 'The Balance of Class Forces in Britain Today', *International Socialism* 2:6, 1979.

2. See D. Lyddon, 'Leyland, Shop Stewards and Participations', *International Socialism* 102, October 1977.

3. T. Cliff, 'Where do we go from here?', *Socialist Review* 1, April 1978.

4. For an analysis of the class struggle during the early Thatcher years see C. Harman, '1984 and the shape of things to come', *International Socialism* 2:29, 1985.

5. See A. Callinicos and M. Simons, *The Great Strike*.

6. T. Cliff, 'Patterns of Mass Strikes', *International Socialism* 2:29, (1985), p. 50.

Chapter 6

1. A. Callinicos, 'Crisis and Class Struggle in Europe Today', *International Socialism* 62 (1994).

2. E. Rose and T. Wooley, 'Shifting Sands? Trade Unions and Productivity at Rover Cars', *Industrial Relations Journal* 23, (1992)

3. R. Croucher, *Engineers at War*, (London 1982), p. 33. See also ibid., 32-6.

4. F. Dobbs, *Teamster Rebellion*, (New York 1972).

5. For more on this see A. Callinicos, 'The Rank and File Movement Today', *International Socialism* 2:17 (1982), pp. 22-5.

6. *Financial Times*, 30 September, 19994.

7. See T. Cliff, 'Patterns of Mass Strikes', *International Socialism* 2:29, (1985).

8. See A. Callinicos and M. Simons, *The Great Strike*, ch. 5.